DIRECTIVE TEACHING
of Children with Learning and Behavioral Handicaps

THOMAS M. STEPHENS

Associate Professor of Education
University of Pittsburgh

DIRECTIVE
TEACHING
of Children with
Learning and Behavioral
Handicaps

CHARLES E. MERRILL PUBLISHING COMPANY
Columbus, Ohio   *A Bell & Howell Company*

1 2 3 4 5 6 7 8 9 10-75 74 73 72 71 70

Printed in the United States of America

Preface

This text is addressed to teachers, prospective teachers, and other professional school personnel who are concerned with managing and instructing children who present educational and behavioral limitations. It is written with the understanding that learning involves behavior and that the two are, in practice, inseparable.

Traditional descriptions of children with learning handicaps have included the notion of a discrepancy between an estimate of intellectual potential and actual level of academic performance. Those with behavioral problems have been variously presented as possessing emotional disorders, social maladjustments, or biological deficits.

Considerable attention has been directed toward hypothetical or suspected causes of maladapted behavior and learning dysfunctions. Typically, the focus is on characteristics of children who display such problems with a search for a relationship between characteristics and dysfunctions. Concerns of this nature may have value to other practitioners but they provide little assistance to teachers who are responsible for managing and instructing these children.

Behaviorally handicapped children are viewed here as those who emit inappropriate responses and display poor or weak control of behavior. The frequency and intensity of their responses are either too great, too little, or bizarre.

Learning handicapped children are presented as being immune to standard academic instruction. One or more of their receptive-expressive modalities may be defective, interfering with reception of information and/or expression of that skill or information which was acquired. In other instances, they may display problems of attention, motivation, or retention.

Teaching can be viewed from at least three perspectives. One is a study of how children learn. Implied here is that children do learn through approaches used in directive teaching. As teachers acquire more knowledge about how children learn they may be better equipped to teach. However, the span is sometimes great between *knowing* how to teach well and *teaching* well. By not emphasizing how children learn, there is no intent to convey the notion that an understanding of this area of scientific inquiry is unimportant. But it is outside the realm of this text.

A discussion of lesser importance is how to effect change in learners through a change in subject matter, such as occurs in the new math, Initial Teaching Alphabet, or other structural forms that seek to improve learning through comprehensive changes in content. Subject matter is not central to the purposes of this text.

How teachers teach is a third consideration and the one that is emphasized here. The focus is on teacher behavior: how they relate to children; how they assess children; how they manage children; and how they teach.

Contents of this book are based upon the assumption that the reader is knowledgeable about two facets of teaching. First that he is familiar with the developmental sequences of academic skills; the sequences of reading, arithmetic, and language skills. Second, the reader is expected to have an understanding of curricula used at the various age-grade levels.

The purposes of this text are as follows:

1. to provide readers with an instructionally relevant orientation to teaching children with learning and behavioral handicaps.
2. to present a way of thinking about teaching that is designed to assist readers in responding systematically to such children.
3. to present an approach to teaching and managing children who display learning and behavioral problems.
4. to systematize an approach, derived primarily from reinforcement theory, that will enable educational practition-

ers to teach handicapped children as well as to improve their social behavior.

I wish to acknowledge the helpful comments of Professors Jack W. Birch and Godfrey D. Stevens, my colleagues at the University of Pittsburgh, who read the entire manuscript in its original form and to Dr. John Yeager who suggested changes in some portions of Chapter 7. Mrs. Jane Burger and Mrs. Barbara Cass helped in the preparation of the Glossary and Index. Mrs. Linda Langley typed this manuscript, for which I am most appreciative.

Pittsburgh, Pennsylvania
June, 1969

THOMAS M. STEPHENS

To the memory of my father Thomas Stephens
and to my beloved wife Evelyn.

Contents

Introduction

Special educators have been concerned for
many years with attempts to individualize the **ONE**
instruction of children who have physical, mental, and emotional
handicaps. These attempts are reflected in the remedial and corrective instruction that occurs through full-time special classes,
part time special classes or resource rooms, and itinerant services.

When engaged in remediation of learning deficits, both special
education teachers and remedial teachers have similar goals. Too
often, however, these two educational services are inadequate and
special or remedial instruction is provided only for those select
children who can meet the supposedly essential qualifications of
either service.

Recently it has become apparent to some special educators that
children who are selected for remedial instruction need to meet
only behavioral criteria rather than standards based on assumptions
or hypothetical constructs. Special education teachers now recognize that instruction results in marked changes in functioning for
many children. These teachers correct inappropriate social and
academic responses in addition to teaching new responses.

Because these teachers view their roles as including remedial
activities, children who previously would have been destined to
spend their school lives entirely in special classes or special schools

are now being returned to general education programs for some portion, if not all, of their school day.

It is important to keep in mind those settings and organizational schemes designed to facilitate the instruction of children with problems of learning and behavior. Teaching as described in this book is with small groups of children either in special class settings or in tutorial roles. In some instances, the children are enrolled in regular classes but receive part of their instruction in special settings where teachers can devote a portion of their time to individual assessment and instruction. In other cases, teaching occurs with groups of approximately three children within regular classes.

CHARACTERISTICS OF CHILDREN WITH LEARNING AND BEHAVIORAL HANDICAPS

Local, state, and federal agencies have devoted attention and funds toward improving the education of children with behavioral and learning problems. A bureau in the U. S. Office of Education was established in recent years to focus attention on educational needs of handicapped children and to dispense funds for research, teacher preparation, and program development. Most states have personnel in departments of public instruction who assist local educational agencies to develop meaningful programs for such children. School districts of any appreciable size tend to have special education services in an attempt to be responsive to the learning problems of these children.

As each group of children with handicaps is better provided for in schools, additional groupings of children with handicapping conditions seem to appear. Witness the surge in new labels for those more subtle disabilities: *the neurologically handicapped; children with minimal brain dysfunction; the learning disordered child;* and *children with perceptual-motor handicaps.* Clearly such terminology reflects our preoccupation with disability and the disease model, a vestige of the medical era in special education. These terms often include inferences about the causes of handicaps. For example, children labeled *neurologically handicapped* presumably have trouble in school due to body dysfunction.

Classifications that are derived from etiological thinking seldom have educational relevance and do not suggest directions for teaching or for curriculum development. Terminology that is based on the biological conditions of children presents three implications. First, body deficits are assumed to cause inadequate behavior. Second, it suggests that by identifying physical disabilities teachers can change the behavioral responses of children. Third, it equates educational treatment with medical treatment.

One must not negate the importance of etiological and biological considerations with respect to disabling conditions. Such factors may be of the utmost importance for those who engage in prevention of disabilities and certain forms of treatment, but we are concerned here with teaching children who are presented to schools after having acquired the biological factors which are presumed to cause learning and behavioral handicaps.

Teachers instruct and manage children on the basis of overt manifestations. Therefore, they respond to the behavior of children, not to diagnostic labels or medical conditions. Those who teach children labeled as having *minimal brain dysfunction,* for example, typically begin by assessing each child's academic skills in order to establish individual instructional levels. If a child is easily distracted, the teacher attempts to control environmental stimuli as a means of reducing the child's hyperactivity. Similarly, children who are labeled *emotionally disturbed* are managed by teachers in an attempt to accommodate the children's behavior to the learning environment. Teachers would continue to be faced with diverse learning rates and variable behavior among children even if it were possible to classify and group them along clear disability lines.

It should be noted that the term *handicaps* used in the title of this book was chosen because it denotes a particular significance to educators. It is intended to convey the concept of burdens which are imposed on the learner when he is faced with educational situations that cannot be resolved due to his body dysfunction or impairment (Stevens, 1962). Thus, teachers are confronted with the *consequences* of the child's handicap.

Teachers have been oriented toward gathering antecedent information about handicapped children, but teachers must respond to the consequences of these histories. Those who are preoccupied with etiological factors have applied a biological model to what is for teachers a behavioral problem. Because of reasons already mentioned, this discussion of teaching and managing children with learning and behavioral handicaps is not concerned with the biological causes of these problems. The focus of this text is educational; therefore, it is necessary for this discussion to be behaviorally oriented. Consequently, those characteristics that are overt and observable will be emphasized and discussed.

Physical examinations by competent medical practitioners may be helpful for educational planning and it is appropriate to conduct these examinations in schools. Medication and other forms of medical treatment should be applied when needed by qualified medical personnel, but the reasons for such examinations should not be confused with the primary purpose of schooling. School placement and teaching approaches are the functions for which educators are qualified. These are outside the competencies of physicians and other medical practitioners.

Learning is a kind of behavior, and for this reason, learning and behavior are inseparable in teaching. They must be separated here, however, for purposes of discussion. It will be noted that a handicapping condition need not affect both learning and other behaviors in the same child. When behavior is thought of as learned either through experiences or through formal instruction, learning and behavior are identical. When learning is defined as the acquisition of subject matter, a distinction is made between the two.

Characteristics of Learning Handicapped Children

Almost all children, at sometime in their lives, exhibit learning problems or display inappropriate behavior; but those who demonstrate persistent difficulties in these areas are referred to as handicapped. We are concerned here with children who have either academic learning deficiencies or serious behavioral problems or both. Frequently children who display poor behavior also have academic learning problems.

Underachievement

Academically handicapped children often demonstrate significant discrepancies between their functional intelligence and academic achievement. They are frequently termed *underachievers*, meaning that they achieve below the level at which they appear capable of functioning. Underachievement is a concept that is widely used by educational practitioners, although its meaning is not standardized. It requires designating a standard of expected or predicted achievement and obtaining a measure of present achievement.

Underachievement presumably exists when there is a significant difference between anticipated achievement and actual achievement. Advocates of the concept of underachievement often use a test of intelligence as the criterion measure which is sometimes termed *anticipated achievement*. This prediction is then compared with achievement measures. These take the form of either school marks or scores from tests of academic achievement. After transforming the I.Q. score to a mental age grade placement score or its equivalent, it is compared with a score representative of academic achievement.

Because of the fallibility of tests and because of errors that are inherent in prediction measures, discrepancy scores may simply be a function of the measures rather than a function of the child. As a result, the phenomenon of overachievement occurs when the child's real achievement exceeds his anticipated achievement. Since overachievement can only be the result of measurement error, logic would dictate that many children who can be classified as underachievers on the basis of discrepancy scores may also be victims of prediction error. The concept of underachievement, even when accurate, has limited use for teachers because it merely establishes a condition of school achievement. It does not specify what the individual does not know or is ready to learn.

Children with severe academic learning handicaps exhibit such pronounced problems when confronted with academic tasks that they are readily identifiable and are sometimes, because of their poor academic functioning, mistakenly considered to be mentally retarded. Pseudo-mental retardation can be viewed as another form of underachievement. Such a condition exists when the child's intellectual functioning is depressed. Results of tests purporting to measure academic aptitude suggest limited intelligence for pseudo-retardates. In such instances, when it can be established that the child has been known to perform at an average level or better, it is reasonable to assume that he is "underfunctioning." Children who bear physical stigmata, display aberrant behavior, function at a low level on achievement tests, and respond poorly to tests of intelligence may be underfunctioning. Some may have innate potential sufficient for them to function at higher intellectual levels given intensive special instruction.

This is not to say that true conditions of mental retardation are not present among large numbers of children who are so diagnosed. But it is important to note that tests are fallible and that diagnostic terms should not dissuade teachers from their primary responsibility to teach children irrespective of test predictions.

Tests for Teaching / Tests as typically used in schools have limited instructional value because scores are often emphasized to the exclusion of responses to items. Tests of intelligence and achievement based on age-grade norms are relevant when the purpose is to determine the relative performance of each child as compared to an equivalent group. These instruments are often constructed for purposes of prediction and are valuable when considering school placement or describing groups. Scores obtained from these tests however, give teachers few clues that can be used for the instruction of children who have learning problems.

It is possible to obtain instructionally valuable information about a student's performance from tests even though they are designed for other purposes. By analyzing responses to items, teachers can extract specific information to be used in teaching. Examples of such tests and ways to use them are found in Chapter Four.

Carefully designed teacher constructed tests provide highly specific information that has immediate application for teaching. Those that are administered prior to a new unit of study, identify children who have not mastered prerequisites needed for comprehension of new material. Tests that cover the content of a lesson that has been completed reveal which concepts must be retaught to which children.

Teachers must often answer questions about individual children that are not readily answerable from results of prediction tests. Some of these questions include: "Which arithmetical concepts does he know, which does he need to learn?" "Which computational skills has he learned?" "Which work-attack skills is he least sure of?" "Which words has he not yet learned to spell?" Tests that provide ready answers to these and similar questions are referred to as criterion-level tests (Laidlaw, 1967). These provide teachers with information that has revelance to instructional objectives. Results of criterion-level tests inform them as to whether the objectives of a lesson have been met and where further instruction is needed. Tests that are most helpful for teaching yield results that can be readily translated into behavioral terms.

Poor Quality of Achievement

It is not just the phenomenon of poor academic achievement that is noted among learning handicapped children but also the poor quality of achievement. A child who has difficulty with reading may confuse letters of the alphabet (i.e., d and b), he may confuse small

words (ie., they and then, we and me, cut and cup), or he may confuse the sounds of letters and words. Arithmetical processes may be
uneven; skill in computation may be adequate with one type of
process but exceedingly poor with an equivalent computational
process.

Basic prerequisites for formal schooling are often found to be
defective in the repertoires of learning handicapped children. These
may include:

–failure to read consistently from left to right
–exceedingly short attention span
–poor recall of previously learned material
–erratic academic performance; knowledge of a process one day
    and failure to use the same skill subsequently
–failure to obey simple directions
–aberrant behavior
–over-reactions to stimuli
–difficulty in counting objects
–poor discrimination of likenesses and differences among objects
    and sounds
–unwillingness to attempt new tasks
–failure to participate appropriately in group activities.

Resistence to Conventional Instruction

In addition to the poor qualitative aspects of achievement, resis-
tence to conventional instruction is often observed. Some students
simply do not profit from standard methods of teaching. While a
majority of their classmates progress academically, they fail to demonstrate gains in spite of average or better intelligence.

Problems in retention of learning are at times noted. Learning
may appear to have occurred but in subsequent observations few
traces of learning remain. Consequently, the child, his teachers, and
his parents soon become discouraged with his slow progress.

Learning handicapped children often view school activities as
unpleasant, for it is in this setting where many of their failure experiences occur. As the cycle of failure persists, they become less
responsive to attempts at teaching and more fearful of academic
tasks. This fear is often reflected in their dislike for school. Typically
they become reluctant learners, unwilling to change. Because of
obvious failures, their peers focus on them and are quick to notify
each other and the teachers of their short-comings. Behavioral and

academic expectations for them are low and they soon begin to view themselves as inadequate, living only by the low standards set for them by others.

As failure increases parents usually become more anxious devoting large portions of time with their learning handicapped children in tutorial activities providing further evidence to them of their inability to learn. They may be taken to all available clinics for diagnosis and therapy. Parents who have the financial resources seek services of a variety of medical specialists hoping that corrective lenses, special exercises, medication, or all of these will eradicate learning handicaps. Unfortunately, persistence by parents usually results in draining family financial and emotional resources and very often contributes little to improved academic performance of learning handicapped children.

Little is known about adults of average or higher intelligence who presented severe learning difficulties while in school. Although, many clinicians and teachers cite personal experiences with such children whom they later knew as adults. Those who by adulthood have not overcome their learning handicaps are believed to adopt a style of living that relies on non-academic skills and seem to avoid occupations that require schooling.

Characteristics of Behaviorally Handicapped Children

Behavior occurs as a part of living with each child learning a personal style of behavior in response to environmental conditions. Various theories have been advanced to account for maladaptive behavior. Some psychological explanations are based on hypothetical constructs believed to be internal to the organism. Others are rooted in biological explanations, while some theories account for all forms of behavior through a combination of learning and inheritance.

Irrespective of the bases for behavioral problems, teachers must respond to handicapped children in terms of their outward manifestations. Those whose responses interfere with their adjustment to school present problems that can be classified into two overlapping areas: 1) children whose rate of behavior interferes with learning, and 2) those whose weak control of behavior interferes with learning. Implied in these categories is the notion that rate of emission and control of behavior affects behaviorally handicapped children's learning as well as that of their classmates. These two categories of behavioral problems are discussed below.

Defects in Rate of Behavior

Children respond in different ways to similar stimuli. Identical conditions may evoke conflicting responses from children in the same classroom and, on occasion, from the same child at different times. Consequently, teachers find in one group children who emit too much behavior and children who emit too little behavior. Further, an over-emission and under-emission of behavior may be displayed by one child under different conditions.

Over-Emission of Behavior

Children who are over-emittors of behavior have been variously described as restless, attention-seeking, disruptive, boisterous, hyperactive, disobedient, overly aggressive, and unruly (Quay, 1968). Their behavior styles preclude effective school adjustment since teachers frequently devote a major portion of their time in response to disruptive behavior. Attention gained by the misbehavior often reinforces undesired behavior and teachers, by their reactions, often inadvertently encourage reoccurrance of misbehavior. Disruptive behavior in school is characterized by distractibility, excessive talking, and aggression towards persons and things.

Distractibility has been commonly associated with the "Strauss Syndrome" (Stevens and Birch, 1957) another label for a certain class of brain-injury. Children who display this behavior are easily distracted by extraneous stimuli and have difficulty focusing on the essentials of a task. Thus, reactions to wrong stimuli result in poor attention.

Excessive talking presents problems to teachers when it annoys other children and when it seriously affects the teaching-learning process. Teachers confronted with such behavior often resort to using various forms of punishment in an attempt to extinguish talking.

Aggression toward property is reflected by inappropriate reactions as observed in children who engage in stealing and damaging property. Defacement of school facilities and instructional materials are behaviors also included in this category.

Under-Emission of Behavior

Children who under-behave have been labeled as quiet, shy, withdrawn, phobic, and autistic. Their most pronounced characteristic is the limited amount of emitted observable behavior. Teachers of such children must choose between ignoring the quiet ones and supporting their behavior, or attempting to elicit responses which may result in inappropriate reactions or further withdrawal.

Teachers have been criticized for their failure to recognize serious maladjustments of children who tend to withdraw (Wickman, 1928; Yourman, 1932). They are inclined to respond to those children who display disruptive behavior and to overlook withdrawn or quiet youngsters because those who are not disruptive do not demand attention from their teachers. Recent studies, however, indicate that teachers are becoming more aware of withdrawn behavior (Hunter, 1957; Ellis and Miller, 1963).

Inhibited Behavior / Rather than risking ridicule, the inhibited child withdraws from interactions with others. Inhibition, in some instances, varies with the conditions under which the child functions. He may be reluctant to participate in school related activities but may emit behavior at an acceptable level out of school. Or in the presence of particular individuals, he may be more inhibited. Extreme cases of inhibition are noted among so-called phobic children where objects, animals, situations, or people may evoke fear responses from these children (Rachman, 1968).

While most teachers are not confronted with extreme cases of inhibition, shyness and lack of responsiveness are more common. The shy child is characterized by partial inhibition of the usual form of behavior when in the presence of others. Teachers find shy children management problems when they are approached because they tend to retreat and because their shyness becomes more pronounced when attention is directed toward them. Their reluctance to participate in group activities and unwillingness to reach out into the environment restricts their learning opportunities. Because learning is accelerated through interaction with others as well as with objects in the environment, those who withhold their responses limit their learning opportunities. As they persist in their withdrawn behavior, few overt responses are expected of them and their unresponsiveness is reinforced.

Weak Control of Behavior

Quality of control is another dimension of behavior that can impair classroom adjustment. At times, children present problems of learning when the rate of emitted behavior is within the normal range but when the control of behavior is inappropriate. In other instances, a child is found to be an underachiever and an over- or under-emitter of behavior, and additionally has impaired behavioral control. At this point in our discussion, problems of behavioral control will be discussed apart from these other handicapping conditions.

Observable characteristics of children with poor control of behavior include: bizarre thinking as reflected in peculiar behavior; problems of attending behavior; impaired social behavior; and unwarranted emotional responses.

Bizarre thinking is noted sometimes in verbalizations of children. They may reply to questions by presenting answers that are clearly unrelated or, they may attempt to participate in a discussion by inserting comments that do not in any way relate to the topic. Other peculiarities of speech may be grunts or animal-like sounds. Such behavior is of sufficient duration and frequency to be outside the normal range of attention seeking behavior. Inflexible attitudes toward others and toward tasks may also be the result of peculiarities in thinking. Children who, in spite of reality, insist on rigidly maintaining that others are to blame for their behavior are engaging in impaired thinking and present barriers to their learning.

Problems of attention occur when children focus on irrelevancies rather than on the point of an assignment or topic. Since attentional acts require the facility to be selective when searching for relevant stimuli, inattentive children are freqeuntly found to be attending to inconsequential trivia. Children who show difficulty in attending to relevant stimuli also are considered to have learning or behavioral handicaps.

Inadequate social behavior is commonly seen among children who are insensitive to their peers and consequently fail to interact appropriately. Such children may refuse to share objects, working space, or discussion time. They tend to engage in self aggrandizement at the expense of others. Even when they do not need additional margins for success, these children may cheat and use other unfair advantages in order to appear superior to their peers and to gain their teacher's favor.

Failure to relate to others at more than a superficial level is also a hallmark of social maladjustment. Children who do not form close relationships with others and who lack deep emotional feelings about their family, peers, or friends are seriously hindered in their social adjustments.

Unwarranted emotional responses are seen in children who cry for seemingly trivial reasons, such as failing to get sufficiently high marks on tests or being asked to respond to questions that they cannot answer. Children who refuse to attempt difficult tasks because of fear of failure and those who sink into withdrawn silence are showing inadequate behavioral control. Rash children, those who act without due consideration, fail to control their emotions because of impetuous behavior. They may be impudent with their teachers, parents, and classmates. It may not be so much that they respond too frequently in a rude manner but that on those occasions in which they are responsive they are inconsiderate.

CASE STUDIES

Mark, an example of underachieving, over-emitting behavior

Mark, an 8 year old male, is repeating second grade. A recent psychological evaluation indicated that he has normal learning potential for his age

School Achievement

At the close of first grade following two years in school, kindergarten and first grade, Mark was reading at a pre-primer level. He was promoted to grade two because of his size and his parents unwillingness to accept his retention. As he began second grade, he had forgotten the few reading skills that he had acquired in first grade. Consequently, he was the poorest reader in his class.

In an attempt to help Mark, the school principal arranged to have him go to first grade daily for reading instruction while he remained enrolled in second grade. He was again exposed to first grade reading material using the same texts that were used with him the previous year. It was noted that, while Mark recalled the pictures, he read the stories so haltingly that one would not have believed that he had prior exposure to them.

Mark's manuscript writing was not good. He often confused *m* with *n* and *d* with *b* as he did in reading. Cursive writing was less confusing but his papers were filled with smudges and smears and were sloppy.

Mark fared no better in arithmetic. Although he did recognize numbers to 10, he could not add correctly beyond one plus one. He was unable to subtract.

By the close of second grade, Mark was reading in a first grade primer and continued to confuse letters and small words. At this point, he was retained in second grade.

Behavior

Mark has a history of erratic behavior; at times he is overly active while at other times he behaves in an acceptable manner.

At play, he becomes noisy and boisterous. He is uncoordinated and has many accidents on the playground. He tends to ignore the rules. Consequently, he is often chosen last by his playmates for team activities.

His classroom behavior is characterized by sudden bursts of energy; he races around the room yelling and shouting, when excited. His teachers have reported frequent inattention which has been variously described as "daydreaming and disinterest." But, as the noise level of the class rises so does Mark's hyperactivity.

At home, his parents report that he often goes to bed at the end of day exhausted and goes quickly to sleep. But during his waking hours, however, he is overly active in the home and in the neighborhood. He is described as somewhat destructive by his mother. She indicates that few objects remain intact after they have been exposed to Mark. He recently dismantled but failed to put together his new two-wheeled bicycle. His new clothing is quickly torn.

Mark is an example of a youngster with a learning handicap. His intelligence, as measured by the Stanford-Binet, is well within the average range (I.Q. 107). Yet, he functions much like a child with less ability. After three years of school (kindergarten, first and second grades), his reading achievement remains at a beginning first grade level. His reading failure appears to be immune to conventional methods and materials. Witness the efforts to teach and reteach him reading using the same basal materials and standard teaching methods.

He repeated one grade in school and, unless he soon begins to master basic reading and arithmetic skills, he can look forward to additional years of failure and frustration. His school experiences could result in negative feelings toward academic learning, a poor self concept, feelings of rejection, and diffused hostility toward society. At the legal age for leaving school, he could find himself out of school, out of work, and ill-equipped for our highly technical society. Yet, Mark is not mentally retarded; his I.Q. score exceeds 66 percent of the population.

Mark's behavior, while not viciously directed towards property and others, is disruptive and does result in physical damage to both himself and to objects. At times, his behavior can be labeled as hyperactive. Note the yelling and other disruptive behavior exhibited by him in the classroom. Distruction of property which may be attributed to carelessness probably exposes him to frequent reprimands at home as well as in school.

Had he been diagnosed by other specialists, Mark might have been termed "minimally brain damaged" by a neurologist; or "emotionaly disturbed" by a psychologist. While such information may be of interest to his teachers, it would provide them with no instructionally relevant information. In fact, it could serve to dissuade them from focusing on more valuable bits of information.

Joan, an example of underachieving, under-emitting behavior

Joan is 12 years, 1 month old and in sixth grade. She was referred to the school psychologist because of low academic achievement and feelings of rejection. Her mother reports that Joan has been depressed since the death of her father 18 months ago. Results of the Revised Stanford-Binet, Form L-M yielded a mental age of 14-10 and an I.Q. of 119.

School Achievement

She was considered an above-average student prior to her father's death. Since that time, her school marks have been dropping and her daily work is now below average. Achievement test results indicated that reading comprehension is at a beginning 4th grade level and reading word recognition at a late 4th grade level. Arithmetic computation was also at an early 4th grade level.

Behavior

Joan's teacher reports that she is extremely quiet in school. She exhibits little interest in other children and appears to have no close friends among her classmates. She is compliant, following all directions, but she never volunteers during class discussion.

Her mother describes Joan's behavior at home similarly. She prefers to stay at home and does not have any close friends. She spends most of her time at home in her bedroom watching T.V. Her 17 year old sister has a close relationship with her and occasionally they go together to a neighborhood theater.

Joan's underachievement is clearly evidenced by the discrepancy between her grade placement and her performance on achievement tests. Her school achievement problems are pronounced in view of her above average intellectual functioning. Her lack of interest in others can be viewed as a serious behavior problem. She emits such little behavior that it is difficult for others to develop a meaningful relationship with her.

It may be accurate to view Joan as an emotionally disturbed child because she appears withdrawn. Many authorities would attribute her poor academic achievement to her emotional depression. Such a cause-effect relationship may be justified. However, to Joan's teacher, inferring or verifying causes of her difficulties would be of little importance with respect to the problem of assisting Joan to be a happy person and a better student.

Lester, and example of poor behavioral control

Lester is a 12 year old boy who was referred by his teacher for psychological testing because of his strange behavior. The school psychologist reported that Lester has normal intelligence in the average range.

School Achievement

Lester is presently in the sixth grade where his teacher reports that he is an average student. School records indicate that he has repeatedly obtained C marks. He has never been retained in school.

Behavior

His teacher has noted that Lester emits animal sounds. Since the beginning of this school year, she has noticed that he often squeals like a pig, or meows, or barks like a dog. He had been seated towards the rear of the room earlier in the year. She assigned him to a front seat in order to observe him after the first month in sixth grade, but the animal-like sounds have continued. Lester seems to be oblivious to his classmates. When his noises are called to his attention, he refrains for a time from such behavior.

Children have reported, in recent weeks, that Lester growls and barks at them on the playground. One second grade girl was frightened by him when he tried to bite her on the leg as she walked to school.

Lester has two younger siblings, a ten year old sister in fifth grade, and a five year old sister at home. His parents have been uncooperative toward the school and to date have refused to come to school for a conference or to permit school representatives to visit their home.

The school psychologist assessed Lester's emotional adjustment as revealed by his responses to a projective test. He found that Lester presents a picture of an extremely immature boy with some regressive tendencies. He appears to be quite insecure, probably because of emotional deprivation; he feels unloved and rejected. He views his world in a distorted fashion. There is also considerable confusion concerning his sexual identification; he seems to identify more with animals and with things than with people.

Lester presents behavioral problems that interfere greatly with his present school placement. His bizarre behavior is potentially dangerous to other children. Certainly, his social adjustment is markedly impaired. His academic achievement has not been seriously affected, although his daily work and school marks are somewhat below his intellectual functioning.

Medically, Lester might be diagnosed as suffering from childhood schizophrenia or some other psychosis. He might be in need of therapy in conjunction with academic instruction. His teacher, however, must relate to his responses in the process of teaching him.

Although Joan, Mark, and Lester exhibit learning and behavioral difficulties their teachers are faced with different problems when teaching them. Joan's lack of expressed responses and her failure to grapple with the environment require her teacher to elicit desirable behavior from her, yet her teacher must be careful not to confront Joan in such a way that she would become more fearful and less responsive. At first, tasks requiring little persistence and almost guaranteeing success should be presented in order to obtain reactions from her.

Mark needs "settling down" and support for behavior which is desirable. Teachers, when confronted with overly active children, often devote their time to reacting to undesirable behavior. Consequently, the child may associate teacher attention with misbehavior. Mark's teacher should identify behavioral areas where he performs appropriately and encourage him to continue these responses and ignore, as often as possible, undesirable behavior.

Lester's evident inability to control his emotions has resulted in serious school management problems. While he probably needs other forms of treatment, in addition to education, certain strategies by his teacher can help him to behave in a more socially acceptable manner.

The future for the Marks, Joans, and Lesters in our schools is much brighter today than it was just a short time ago. School personnel are more sensitive to children with learning and behavioral handicaps. Teachers are better equipped to individualize their teaching styles and numbers of special programs are increasing in order to identify, remediate, and return children to general education. Subsequent chapters in this book focus on a way of thinking about such children. Assessment procedures are suggested for gathering instructionally relevant information, and approaches that aid in their management and teaching are described.

Summary

Concern for educating children with learning and behavioral handicaps has increased rapidly in recent years. This concern is reflected by an increase in school programs and efforts at national, state, and local levels in behalf of such children.

Special education teachers are shifting their activities away from the traditional goals which have existed for many years toward an emphasis on returning more children to general education. This trend requires remedial instruction for selected handicapped children.

Children with learning and behavioral handicaps are characterized by underachievement; poor quality of achievement; resistance to conventional instruction; defects in rate of behavior; and weak control of behavior. These characteristics are purposely presented in observable terms in an attempt to make them relevant for teachers.

Teaching: The Manipulation of Variables

A competent teacher of children, and particularly children with learning and behavioral problems, has a thorough understanding of the learning process. Teachers should remember that those who provide advice about teaching, even well-intended individuals who are specialists in other professions, without the preparation and experience of a teacher are at best subordinate to the teacher.

TWO

The primary purpose for placing children in schools is for educating them, but school placement also involves some secondary purposes for students. These include: socialization; maintenance of sound mental and physical health; remediation of physical and mental deficits; and development of positive self-concepts. In school environments however, these generally serve to buttress the academic functioning of children. A medical examination, for instance, that is provided under the auspices of the school serves to locate and, if followed by treatment, to alleviate physiological barriers to learning. But examination and treatment need not necessarily be conducted in a school setting and should not be viewed as a part of the children's schooling or part of the educational process.

In school, the teachers are the central specialists. They perform those basic services for which schools exist. Other professionals who are school employees, or who render information about the child, form the corp of assistants to the teachers. Their behavior should be different in school than it would be in a setting in which their services were primary. They should not view teachers as serving as their aides or as individuals available to carry out their prescriptions.

Teachers should know which services other professionals can provide and the limits of their services. They should not expect or seek leadership from non-educators with respect to educational problems. Some professionals not prepared to teach, in the past, have viewed themselves as experts in all human affairs due to their presumed superior professional standing and years of schooling. It was common for physicians to advise teachers and parents as to teaching procedures. Today, however, educators are well prepared to teach, although some teachers may be perpetuating the mistaken belief that others are equally competent by encouraging unqualified individuals to usurp their roles.

Lester, in Chapter One, was believed to be in need of psychotherapy. If the therapist is employed in the school, he provides adjunctive services for teachers. Thus the teacher may, if desired, refer Lester for therapy or for further psychological study through appropriate channels as designated by school policy.

However, it would be inappropriate for the therapist to prescribe therapeutic activities to be used by the teacher with Lester since the teacher's function is educational. Because Lester is in school, the teacher is not the therapist's agent. Just as the teacher is not competent to recommend therapeutic approaches, the therapist is without protocol to recommend teaching methods.

THREE VARIABLES

Those who view teaching as easy often see it as merely imparting information. It is, rather, a highly sophisticated process in which situations must often be contrived in order for learning to occur. Successful teaching involves using strategies and manipulating three important variables. Each is essential to teaching-learning situations and each overlaps the others. These variables are:

1. instructional media
2. school environments, and
3. student behavior.

The remainder of this chapter will be devoted to an elucidation of these three variables.

Instructional Media

The burst of new technology has made an impact on teaching. We not only have more effective and more appealing printed materials, but we have a large array of electronic devices to aid us in our teaching.

Some of these materials are designed to be used in conjunction with a particular method or are predicated upon certain assumptions about the learning process. Witness the printed matter for teaching reading. Cards, charts, and stories are available to teachers who use the "sight method" or the "phonetic method." Although the "kinesthetic method" for teaching reading is not as easily built into software or hardware, even this method has been purported to be a part of commercially obtained instructional materials.

Types of Instructional Media

One way to classify instructional media is from the point of view of teacher use. From this perspective, the classification scheme includes at least two types:

1. media designed for control by teachers and
2. media designed to control the method of presentation.

Instructional media that are designed for control by teachers are commonly used in schools. Contents of this type, when commercially prepared, are usually presented in a sequential fashion, building on concepts that were either previously presented in a series or were assumed to have been learned at another time. One characteristic is that the methodology to be used for instruction is left to teachers. A rationale for ways in which the authors believe children will most effectively learn the content, however, may be reflected in either accompanying teacher manuals or in the manner in which content is presented.

Basal reading texts and correlated workbooks are prime examples of this type of material in printed form. Repetition of new words and other techniques for vocabulary control are often incorporated into these texts, but teachers are not confined to the use of any particular approach in order to get maximum use from these materials.

Media that permit control by teachers are not restricted to printed material. Audio-visual aids are frequently available for use with printed material and seldom restrict the teaching methods to be used. Teaching aids that can be selected to supplement instruction also fit this category.

Teachers may make their own media in lieu of commercial material or to enrich existing modes of instruction. Teacher constructed materials have been used longer than any other as a means of individualizing instruction. Until recent years, before publishers were oriented toward the exceptional child, teachers often found it necessary to devise special material for children with learning problems. They often collect pictures, and magazine and newspaper clippings to be used in constructing instructional materials.

Teachers may create their own flash cards for teaching word recognition and computation and for other drill games. Work sheets are often made for use by selected children who are in need of additional practice or who have other special needs that are not readily met through using standard materials. With increasing use of instructional material centers, films and slides are being designed by teachers and constructed to their specifications.

Media designed to control methods of presentation contain a pre-designed methodology. These are predicated upon assumptions that the built-in methods are essential to effective learning of materials within the framework of the medium.

Some materials have incorporated a modified alphabet into the printed text in an attempt to make reading more easily mastered. In other instances, printed symbols may be paired with color so as to emphasize specific sounds or word structure.

Modern mathematics is an example of how methodology becomes a part of instructional materials. The new mathematics has generated numerous printed materials none of which is of much value if used to teach traditional arithmetic. One should not assume, however, that because commercially prepared texts advocate certain methods for children, with or without handicaps, that they are superior to other printed matter or methods (Kline, 1966).

Teacher constructed materials may also contain embedded methodology, depending upon measures of flexibility permitted in responding to the media. Even experience charts, to some extent, control children's reactions and dictate modes of presentation. Teachers, for example, who design seat work requiring students to match the numbers of objects in a picture to a number symbol are to a large extent controlling the method of presentation.

Similarly, a silent film strip that is designed to teach the association of symbols to sounds is an example of a visual aid that relies on one sensory channel.

Programmed instruction is a prime example of embedded teaching methods. These auto-instructional materials are designed to provide immediate feedback to learners about the accuracy of their responses. The instructional material is broken down into minute steps so that students can progress from basic to more complex tasks with a minimum of failure. Programmed texts leave little room for teachers to modify the presentations of subject matter, although teachers are free to supplement programmed instruction.

Knowledge of Students and Media

Teachers of children with learning and behavioral handicaps are confronted with major requirements when they choose instructional materials. To select relevant media, they must have considerable knowledge of their students as well as of the instructional material.

First, it is necessary to have access to information concerning which academic skills already have been acquired by their students. If such information is not available, teachers should be sufficiently skilled in observational and assessment techniques so that they can identify those skills already learned by their students. In order to be able to know what each child can learn next, one must be thoroughly knowledgeable concerning hiearchies of skill development. Without an understanding of skill sequence, one cannot establish accurate instructional goals or outcomes for students.

Second, teachers of such children must also have a knowledge of which sensory modalities are most effective for learning by each child. If such information is not available to them, they must be skilled in assessing sensory-expressive learning.

Third, one must have ready access to a wide variety of instructional media that can be ordered and made available with short notice. Hopefully, the practice of equipping each teacher with instructional materials prior to the knowledge of the instructional needs of each child is vanishing from the schools. It should be replaced by practices that permit quick distribution of needed material *after* teachers have had exposure to those children in need of special instruction.

Prerequisites to Learning

The reader will recall Mark who was used as an example of an under-achiever and an over-emittor of behavior in Chapter One. When selecting materials for teaching reading to Mark, what should his teacher know about him?

His teacher must know what prerequisites to reading he already has acquired. These are:

1. Visual Skills

    Visual Acuity: Does he see well enough to read printing?

    Visual Discrimination: Does he discriminate gross differences between objects, geometric figures, or words? Does he note fine differences between words or letters?

    Eye Movement: Does he move his eyes from left to right? Does he approach reading in a left to right progression?

    Color Discrimination: Does he see differences in colors? Does he attach correct names to various colors?

    Use of Pictures: Does he use pictures contained in the text when reading? Does he describe the details of a picture? Does he accurately interpret meanings of pictures? Does he arrange pictures that relate to a story into an accurate sequence?

2. Speaking and Listening Skills

    Hearing: Is his hearing acuity normal? If he has a hearing loss, does it interfere with reading?

    Sound Discrimination: Does he discriminate gross differences in sound, i.e., high vs. low tones; loud vs. soft sounds; differences in words? Does he discriminate differences among sounds of letters?

    Pronunciation: Does he mispronounce common words? Does he display any other speech defects?

    Speaking Vocabulary: Are words he is expected to read within his speaking vocabulary?

3. Reading Skills

    Letters: Does he recognize and know the names of letters in the alphabet?

    Words: Which basic sight vocabulary words does he readily know?

    Sounding: Does he know all single consonant sounds and consonant blends? Does he sound long vowels and short vowels?

    Syllabication: Which principles of syllabication does he apply?

Signs: Does he demonstrate an understanding of marks that indicate questions, exclamations, pauses, stops, and shifts in speakers?

4. Motor Skills

   Directions: Does he know his right hand from his left hand? Does he know his right foot from his left foot? Does he know differences in positions, i.e., up, down, under, over, above, below, etc.?

   Haptics: Does he feel differences between surfaces? Does he feel differences between temperatures? Does he feel differences between shapes?

5. Attitudes

   Interest in Reading: Does he enjoy being read to? Does he have favorite stories? Does he recall details of a story accurately? Does he look forward with pleasure to reading instruction?

   Assignments: Does he attempt to do assignments relating to reading instruction? Does he follow directions? Does he enjoy doing workbook assignments?

   Attitudes toward Books: Does he have favorite books? Does he show care when handling books?

   Using Reading Skill: Does he use his skills in reading for obtaining information outside of school assignments? Does he distinguish reading for pleasure from reading for information?

These questions, that Mark's teacher should ask concerning his readiness for reading instruction, are stated in behavioral terms rather than inferential terms. His teacher must establish not whether he *can* perform various skills but whether, in fact, he *does*. Answers to these and similar questions will identify for the teacher Mark's strengths and weaknesses with reference to reading and will assist the teacher in selecting appropriate instructional materials for reading. If Mark's teacher had noted, for example, that he did not recognize differences in color, reading material that relied on using color for seeing differences in words should not be selected.

When students do not demonstrate prerequisites for the tasks to be learned, these should be taught prior to presenting the more advanced tasks. Mark's teacher should devise an instructional task or series of tasks for him to learn recognition of colors if he does not recognize differences in color and assuming that he has within his repertory the facility to discriminate colors.

Instructional Purposes

Teachers should have purposes for instruction clearly in mind when choosing media for teaching children. Materials selected for use must be related to instructional outcomes. An analysis of each child's functioning is necessary in order for teachers to specify outcomes.

The following answers to those questions concerning prerequisites for teaching Mark reading will help his teacher establish specific goals for his reading instruction.

Visual Skills / A thorough examination by a vision specialist revealed normal vision. Both near and far point acuity were within the normal range.

Psychological testing and teacher observations indicated that Mark discriminates gross differences among objects and shapes accurately. His level of accuracy dropped, however, when required to make fine discriminations. The school psychologist noted that Mark correctly responded to all ten pictorial similarities and differences at year 5 on the Stanford-Binet.

Mark's teacher found that he confused *w* with *m*; *b* with *d*; *m* with *n*; *p* with *q*; and *was* with *saw*.

Mark does move his eyes from left to right, but he does not consistently read print from left to right. It was noted by both his teacher and the psychologist that at times he attacks words from right to left and may attempt to read lines of print from right to left.

He readily recognizes and properly names basic colors. He tends to rely heavily on pictures for clues to word recognition and reading comprehension and he interprets pictures accurately.

Speaking and Listening Skills / An audiometric examination revealed normal hearing, yet Mark has difficulty discriminating differences among sounds. He confuses the *th* sound with *d*; *bl* with *ba*; and *f* with *v*. His mispronunciation of words is believed to be related to his tendency not to discriminate differences in sounds, thus he tends to pronounce *that* as *dat*.

His speaking vocabulary appears to be above average for his chronological age. A careful check of words found in reading texts used in first grade revealed that all words were well within his speaking vocabulary.

Reading Skills / Mark knows the names of all letters in the alphabet, when presented to him in printed form, with the exception of *m* and *n*; *q* and *p*; and *d* and *b* which he confuses.

He readily recognizes about 100 of the Dolch basic sight vocabulary (Dolch, 1936). The remaining 120 Dolch words have not yet been mastered by him.

His sounding skills are almost nil. Mark sounds many of the initial single consonants but has great difficulty with all consonant blends. He readily sounds long vowels but has trouble with short vowel sounds. He does not demonstrate an understanding of the phonetic principles of syllabication.

Mark does not read with inflection and does not demonstrate or use the various punctuation symbols.

Motor Skills / Mark demonstrates a confusion in handedness; at times he uses his right hand for writing, at other times he writes with his left hand. He is also confused with respect to direction; he is uncertain about *right* and *left*, *up* and *down*, *under* and *over*, *above* and *below*. He does show an understanding of *front*, *back* and *side*.

Mark's haptic sense is not finely developed. He feels gross differences between textures when blindfolded, but he does not correctly identify fine differences between *rough* and *smooth* or *warm* and *cool*.

Attitudes / Despite his repeated failures in school, he has a zest for learning. While he does not like to read, he does enjoy listening to stories and he asks that stories be read or told to him. However, if the span of time for listening exceeds ten minutes Mark begins to lose interest and engages in irrelevant talking and becomes difficult to manage.

Assignments involving reading are difficult for him and he soon engages in inappropriate behavior, but reading readiness activities, such as discrimination of geometric figures and matching letters and words interest him. His tolerance for individual assignments involving reading readiness activities on the average is about 15 minutes within a range of 10 minutes to 20 minutes.

He attempts to read commercial and safety signs and shows a particular interest in words contained in advertisements.

Tasks for Mark

An analysis of the child's functioning will help establish instructional goals for him. For example, the aforementioned information about Mark's skills in reading and prerequisite skills to reading will enable his teacher to establish the following specific instructional outcomes. During the next several weeks, Mark should learn to:

Directionality
–identify his right side
–identify his left side
–indicate over, under, above, below, up, down, right of and left of objects
–read consistently from left to right

Work Habits
–work at individual assignments for average periods of 20 minutes
–listen to stories for periods of at least 20 minutes

Reading Skills
–discriminate the printed symbols *w, m, b, d, p,* and *q*
–read *was* and *saw* correctly
–hear differences between words beginning with *th, d, bl, ba, f,* and *v.*
–recognize an additional 50 Dolch Basic Sight Words
–listen to stories that are read with inflection

Note that instructional outcomes for teaching Mark reading are specified in behavioral terms, rather than in terms that are inferential. We state that Mark should learn to *identify* his right side, as opposed to *knowing* his right side. Thus, we can determine through observations if Mark has learned to *identify* his right from his left, but we cannot observe his *knowing* this concept.

Selection of Instructional Media

It is possible for teachers to select appropriate instructional media for children once outcomes have been specified. Mark's teacher, for example, should select instructional devices for teaching reading to him that are consistent with the outcomes that are noted above. His teacher should systematically apply selected printed matter containing desired words, rather than haphazardly using reading material that may or may not contain the words *was* and *saw*.

Similarly, Mark's teacher could assign him to listen to a tape recording of a story that is read with *inflection*. By carefully matching instructional media with the specified outcomes, teachers can expedite learning and avoid general approaches to specific learning problems.

Mark's teacher should also make a decision concerning instructional media to be used. For example, since Mark does recognize primary colors, his teacher could elect to use reading material that relies on color as a means for teaching initial consonant blends. His teacher could strive toward the goal of improving his tolerance for working on individual assignments. This goal could be met by using programmed material requiring progressively more time to complete each frame. Or, a timing device could be used for gradually increasing the time demands of assignments.

The Instructional Materials Center Network for Handicapped Children and Youth provides services to special educators throughout the United States including Puerto Rico and the Virgin Islands (McCarthy, 1968). These centers lend books and other manipulative materials for review to special education teachers upon request. Some centers have computer programs which permit searching catalogued materials in order to locate items that meet teacher specifications. Presumably, Mark's teacher could request from the nearest instructional materials center reading matter written at a beginning level that contains those instructional tasks indicated above. His teacher could request, for example, workbook material containing exercises that aid in learning the concepts of: over, under, above, below, etc.

With increasing use of specificity in teaching children with learning and behavioral handicaps, cross indexing of catalogued materials will become more prevalent in order to provide the necessary precision when responding to teacher requests.

Manipulation of the School Environment

We try to regulate learners' environments in many ways, the most obvious way is through careful design of school facilities. Schools are purposely made pleasant through attractive architecture, colorful interiors, and comfortable furniture. The intent is to make schools a place where students and teachers enjoy working.

Grouping of Students Within Schools

Conditions are also manipulated to facilitate instruction by organizing school populations. Students have been grouped by age; grade; sex; I.Q.; achievement; course selection; and by handicapping condition. Each basis for grouping has its adherents and its disclaimers. Even though certain organizational schemes have long been used in attempting to individualize instruction, studies assessing effects of organizational patterns are few in number. A few typical studies are reviewed below to illustrate past research.

Studies of Instructional Patterns

Holmes and Harvey (1956) studied six classes of third, fourth, and sixth grade children. Each grade level contained one class that was exposed to a flexible grouping procedure for instruction in arithmetic and another class that was organized into a fixed grouping pattern. Testing at the beginning of the school year and at the close of the school year yielded no significant gains in arithmetic achievement. It was concluded that classroom organization had little influence on academic achievement. The range of achievement increased between low and high I.Q. groups irrespective of grouping method. While this study was concerned with grouping within classrooms, it did demonstrate the importance of controlling I.Q. when studying the effectiveness of instructional organizations.

Holmes and Harvey stated that their results might have been different if classes were grouped by ability levels, rather than merely within classes. They gave no reasons for their belief. One could assume that they felt, with a restricted range of intelligence, grouping within classes would have reduced ability differences sufficiently to result in more effective instruction.

Jones (1948) studied 288 fourth grade students drawn from one large school district. She concluded that children, regardless of intelligence, made higher academic gains in flexible grouping programs than did those in classrooms where no grouping occurred. Students in her treatment group were taught on their individual levels of achievement. The control group was taught the prescribed fourth grade curriculum.

One weakness of Jones' study was that, while she attempted to manipulate one independent variable (grouping), it was likely that she actually manipulated two variables (grouping and curriculum). All of the subjects were from the same school system and, in the case of her control group, were exposed to an identical curriculum. Consequently, those differences in favor of the treatment group may have been the result of a difference in curriculum rather than grouping procedure.

In an early study, Washburne and Raths (1927) found that students who had been in the more flexible Winnetka plan fared better academically than did those students in more conventional programs. They evaluated the high school achievement of students who had participated in the Winnetka Elementary School Program. Comparisons were made with other students in the same high school who had their elementary school instruction in schools other than

Winnetka. Although the mean I.Q. scores for all groups were equal, the students who had attended the Winnetka Elementary School were superior in all academic areas. The lapse of time and the intervening learning between attendance in the Winnetka Elementary School and the evaluation of high school performance is a questionable feature of the study, as well as the evident inability of the investigators to exercise any real control over those groups that came from other elementary schools.

A more recent study (Stephens, 1966) compared the organizational patterns used with partially seeing children in grades five and six. Findings suggest that those differences found among the children were unrelated to placement. Since they probably existed prior to placement, the differences could not be directly attributed to advantages of any organizational scheme.

Findings of studies of organizational patterns for students appear to be inconclusive and often improperly designed. The two studies summarized above showed advantages in favor of programs that geared instruction to individual needs. The other studies did not demonstrate the superiority of any one grouping procedure.

Few studies are found which specifically relate to organizational schemes for the education of handicapped children. A survey of the literature concerned with administration of special education revealed a paucity of studies concerned with advantages or disadvantages of one plan of organization or of comparisons among plans (Dunn, 1963).

It appears that special educators have had to rely on expert opinion, often conflicting, as the basis for determining which plans to adopt for instructing students with learning and behavioral handicaps.

It is likely that studies of organizational schemes purporting to provide for individual differences have been inconclusive because the bases for placing youngsters in groups are not directly related to specific instructional goals. For example, when students are grouped solely on the basis of I.Q. the group has a wide range of youngsters in terms of school achievement and diverse reward systems.

Consequently, while the teacher is faced with a group of children who are similar on one variable (in this instance I.Q.) they may be greatly different on variables that are more important to instruction and classroom management.

Organizational schemes for effective instruction of children with learning and behavioral handicaps should be based upon at least three factors:

1. *Types of Rewards:* Grouping procedures should take into account types of rewards or reinforcement needed by each student in order to provide incentives for change.[1] Those students who require more primitive types of rewards will require different conditions for instruction than will those who respond to other types of reinforcement.

2. *Academic Skills:* Each member of the same group should be achieving beyond a specified level in all skill areas. This will serve to reduce the range of differences in academic functioning which is a relevant variable for instruction.

3. *Duration of Groups:* Special grouping within the school and within a class should be viewed as temporary. Students should be reassigned to other groups as their achievement and reinforcement levels change. Whenever children display sufficient academic skills and appropriate behavior they should be placed in regular classes for at least part of their day.

Control of Classroom Conditions

Teachers attempt to control students within classrooms by modifying environmental conditions. They use special seating arrangements of selected children, grouping for special instruction, and structuring of classroom activities.

Special seating arrangements include screening devices, such as those advocated by Cruickshank *et al.* (1961), for use with children who are hyperactive presumably due to the effects of extraneous visual and auditory stimuli. The child is seated in a situation whereby he is surrounded by three panels. In this position, the teacher has ready access to him and yet he is not easily distracted.

Educators should be aware of possible dangers when screens are indiscriminately used with children who are under-emittors of behavior, such as Joan in Chapter One. Joan obviously would have few chances to emit behavior and her teacher would have little opportunity to elicit behavior from her if she were surrounded by screens.

Special seating arrangements for children with behavioral problems should be based on observable evidence. Teachers should try to determine which features within the environment contribute to disruptive behavior. Environmental conditions that set off misbehavior may consist of other children, requirements of a task, or responses to the child. Such stimuli may serve to start inappropriate reactions, while responses by the teacher as well as by other chil-

---

[1] See Chapter Three for a discussion of rewards and reinforcement.

dren to the misbehavior may reinforce and thus teach the child improper behavior.

Sampling of behavior over a period of time through observational techniques, such as video-tape recorders, can provide base-line information upon which a teacher can make decisions for modifying classroom conditions. It would be desirable for all teachers to have ready access to video-tape equipment for use in studying their pupils' reactions to each other and to instruction.

Grouping for special instruction is widely used by teachers in attempting to facilitate instruction. Teachers many times group children on a permanent basis. Usually this occurs when children are grouped for imprecise purposes based on general information about them, such as reading grade levels or test scores. Long term grouping of this sort fails to recognize individual differences among children in their rates of learning. It also ignores differences in performances that can result in similar test scores; students earning identical scores may pass and fail different test items.

Grouping on a temporary basis should be generally viewed as more desirable than permanent or long-term grouping since the latter types of grouping tend to reflect a lack of specificity for instruction. Small groups may be organized on a short-term basis for purposes of teaching a particular skill. In such an instance, all youngsters in the group would have been assessed as being ready to learn the skill, but as not yet having acquired it.

Since learning rates of children vary widely, some group members will readily advance through one special group, having quickly achieved the instructional goal. They may be placed in other groups formed for purposes of specific, short-term instruction. Other children may be members of special groups over longer periods of time because their mastery of the goal requires additional time.

In general, grouping for instruction within classrooms should be based upon immediate teaching objectives. Regrouping should be a common practice.

Structuring of classroom activities is another means teachers use when attempting to control classroom conditions. It involves structuring physical space as well as time. Classroom space may be used for structuring activities by establishing a listening center in a particular area where children may go to engage in audio activities, and browsing may be restricted to an area where supplementary reading materials are stored.

Time is structured by designating certain periods during the school day when particular actvities will occur. Some teachers begin each day by presenting to the students a schedule of the day's activities. Other teachers alternate difficult activities with easier ones by using timing devices or through scheduling procedures.

By structuring in these ways teachers can conduct academic instruction and still allow for other learning activities with a minimum of interference to other students.

Manipulation of Human Behavior

Manipulation of human behavior is the essence of directive teaching and is viewed here as the primary purpose of special instructional programs for children with learning and behavioral handicaps. The previously described variables, instructional media and environmental control, are less direct means toward control of students.

Direct manipulation of human behavior takes place as result of rewarding responses. All reactions of children beyond certain visceral ones have been learned. They learn to like or dislike particular activities in school; they learn styles of behavior; they learn to respond to a given stimulus in a given fashion; and they learn that the sum of 2 + 2 is 4. In short, children behave as they do because of how they have learned to respond.

Teachers devote a great deal of their time to group and individual control. They establish rules for behavior and mete out varying degrees of punishment for infractions of rules of conduct. They attempt to forestall misbehavior by carefully regulating the school day so that students have little opportunity to be idle and to engage in disruptive behavior.

Management of student behavior is also used by teachers in order to improve academic learning. Experienced teachers have long recognized that behavior adjustment is one important prerequisite to school learning. Many believe that children who follow directions poorly and who cannot attend for reasonable periods of time derive less from schooling than do those who maintain attention and who carry out instructions correctly. Thus, manipulation of learners is necessary for two related purposes:

1. to manage student behavior and
2. to result in more academic learning.

Management of Student Behavior

Children who exhibit serious problems are particularly difficult to manage and to teach in groups of any size. It is for this reason that frequently when special classes are available for such children teacher-pupil ratios are reduced. In some instances an aide to the teacher is provided to assist in classroom management.

Teachers use a variety of techniques in attempting to control and direct group activities. These are ordinarily ways of getting students to attend to selective stimuli and means for preventing disruptive behavior. Teachers are, in fact, more effective in obtaining and maintaining student attention than are all other visual media (Saettler, 1968).

Attention seeking schemes are often used by successful teachers for purposes of behavior management and instruction. They use these as cues in order to change the pace of an activity, usually to slow it down, and for signalling students that a change in behavior is indicated.

One way to induce a set is to use auditory stimuli, such as a change in voice. Teachers may regulate their voice volumes, raising or lowering as desired. Change in sound serves as a signalling device for calling attention to the originator of the sound. Further, teachers can condition groups to become quiet and to listen when the teacher suddenly stops talking.

Cuing techniques can be used to signal children. If Mark's teacher, for example, wishes to develop the use of his right hand for writing, a signalling system can be arranged between him and his teacher. Mark should be told that it is best for him to write with his right hand only, assuming that such is the case. And, in order to help him, the teacher will remind him not to use his left hand for writing by saying *"ah ah."* At this sound, Mark should cease using his left hand and place the pencil in his right hand.

In order to manage the signalling system, Mark should be seated so that he can easily be seen by the teacher. His teacher should plan to reinforce the use of his right hand through praise or whatever Mark considers to be reinforcing.

It is likely that Mark will more frequently use his right hand for writing than his left hand. Consequently, he will receive more positive reinforcement than negative reminders and will not associate attention with the use of his left hand only.

Other auditory stimuli have been used by teachers in attempting to manage disruptive children. A few notes from the piano may indicate that it is time to change activities. Or, a snap of the teacher's fingers will call attention to a child's inappropriate behavior.

Visual stimuli have also been used by teachers to control student behavior. A change in lighting can be used as a signal for a change in activity. When the light switch is flicked, the children return to their seats and listen for instructions.

Avoidance techniques are used by teachers to prevent disruptive behavior from occurring. By using such approaches teachers anticipate possible difficulties and are able to avoid using negative actions. By reducing the frequency of undesirable behavior, teachers have more opportunities to reinforce desirable responses. Children are given opportunities to associate many positive feelings toward school and toward teachers due to the frequency of positive reinforcement.

Youngsters who are impulsive reactors are assisted in reducing their impulsivity and hyperactivity by being forewarned prior to an event's occurrence, very much like route signs on a road advise drivers that a turn is immediately ahead. For example, the teacher might indicate that:

> When I say *start,* you must go back to your seats
> quietly and begin your arithmetic assignments.

Using anticipatory statements provides disruptive students with lead time to change the pace of their current activities and to get set for a change in behavior. This tactic is particularly valuable when the change in activity requires learners to move to another area of the classroom. By establishing a key word, i.e., *start,* the teacher is establishing an association of a specific word with a specific behavior.

Structuring the entire day's activities at the beginning of the school day is another way to help children anticipate the changes that will be expected during that day. As the teacher describes what events will occur, each major activity should be written on the chalkboard for later reference by the students. If events are numbered in sequence, children can readily note which portion of the day's activities are completed and what is yet to take place.

Facial and eye contact by teachers with individual children serves as an attention getting device that can be used when giving instructions. The technique can be used in a group setting when the teacher is assisting a child who has difficulty in attending to directions. In this case, the teacher captures the child's attention through a prior signaling system. When students are told, "Boys and girls here are your instructions," the child and the teacher make eye contact during verbal instructions.

The same technique can be used in a one-to-one setting where the teacher asks the child to watch and listen while the task to be accomplished is explained.

Control for Improved Instruction

Teachers can control stimuli that will hopefully result in improved responses from learners.

Over-emittors of behavior have a tendency to be impulsive when confronted with a task requiring some degree of consideration. Children like Mark have developed learning styles that are based primarily on trial and error rather than on forethought. Mark, because of his impulsivity, responds unthinkingly and this style of response has become ingrained in his behavior. Consequently, he has not learned to think through problems and he has frequently been discouraged because his responses were often incorrect.

Providing Mark with the answer to a question, prior to asking it, and describing the cognitive steps that must be used to arrive at the correct responses is one technique that can help develop his thinking processes.

The answer to this problem (addition) is 13. Let's see how to get that answer. First draw 8 circles next to the number 8. Now draw 5 circles next to the number 5. How many circles do we have in all?

Later, when the student has become secure in using one means of solving a problem the teacher can present an alternate method that will result in the same answer. Thus, the teacher will have: 1) taught the child to think through problems, and 2) shown the child that different problem solving techniques exist.

Under-emittors of behavior, like Joan, are reluctant to respond to stimuli. Teachers should begin with tasks that are within the children's response repertories and that are sufficiently stimulating so that they will respond. In group settings, teachers might precede questions with reluctant responders' names. It will serve as a forewarning to listeners and provide lead time for planning their responses.

It is necessary, sometimes, to use a prompting technique in order to involve reluctant students in learning situations. This can be done in several different ways. The following dialogue between a teacher and a small reading group demonstrates a prompting technique used after silent reading of a segment of a story:

Teacher: There are two boys in our story today, one is Fred, the other boy's name rhymes with meat. What is his name, Mark?

Mark: Pete

Teacher: That is right, Mark. Fred and Pete are the boys' names. Very good! Now listen. Fred and Pete are having trouble agreeing how to spend their Saturday afternoon. There is a baseball game and a circus in town. Fred wants to go to the baseball game. But Pete wants to go where, Joan?

Joan: To the circus

Teacher: Very good, Joan!

It is evident that the teacher, in the above dialogue, provided enough information to guarantee correct responses. Even if the students failed to comprehend fully what they had read, prompting by the teacher assured success. Note that questions were directed to each student *after* asking. In this way all children in the group anticipate the question and are expected to listen. In instances where the child is obviously not listening, the teacher might announce the student's name prior to posing the question in order to obtain the child's attention. But this technique should not be used too often in group settings since children will tend to lose interest in questions that are not intended for them.

Questions can be asked and also answered by the teacher as a prompt for those who do not know the correct answer. This technique can be used when the questions are too difficult for many of the children, or it can be used when the teacher is not certain which learner knows the answer. In using this tactic, the teacher also provides reinforcement for those who already thought of the correct response. Under these conditions, the teacher should pause before issuance of the answer in order to give those who might know the correct response an opportunity to respond. By gradually delaying the correct answer, the teacher shifts from an emphasis on prompting to an emphasis on reinforcement.

Summary

Competent teaching is a highly intricate act requiring professional training and experience. Teachers should be aware of the limitations of other professionals who work in schools and should recognize that non-educators in the schools are ancillary personnel to teachers.

Teaching involves manipulating instructional media, school environments, and students. Instructional media are designed to be controlled by teachers and/or to control methods of teaching.

In order to select appropriate instructional media, teachers must have information that is relevant to instruction. They must have knowledge of prerequisites for learning specific academic skills, knowledge of skill sequence, and information about the student's performance.

The school environment is controlled through design of physical facilities, special grouping of learners, and procedures within classrooms.

Manipulation of learners is accomplished by cuing students and using techniques that anticipate and prevent disruptive behavior. By rewarding desired responses, teachers can develop new behaviors among their students.

Principles of Learning for Teachers

Chances are great that large num- **THREE**
bers of teachers have been influ-
enced, either directly or indirectly, by doctrines of depth psycholgy.
In being prepared to teach, they were taught, or they inferred from
what they were taught, that children with adjustment or learning
problems are evidencing symptoms of deep seated neuroses (Kubie,
1958; Fenichel, 1945). Selected citations from psycho-analytically
oriented writers exemplify this orientation.

> The oral inhibitions may be displaced onto other activities with
> a hidden oral significance, such as drinking and smoking, social
> activities, or reading.[1]

> The particular subject, or something associated with the first
> instruction in this subject, or the personality of the teacher and
> his way of teaching, or an accidental feature that essentially had
> nothing to do with the subject proper, like a particular number
> in mathematics or a particular letter in reading or writing, proved
> to be associated with fundamental conflicts around infantile sex-
> uality.[2]

---

[1] Otto Fenichel, *The Psychoanalytic Theory of Neurosis* (New York: W. W.
Norton & Company, Inc., 1945), p. 175.
[2] *Ibid.*, p. 181

> First among them is the child who in his struggle with author-
> ity becomes an obsessional dawdler. This may begin in the nur-
> sery in dawdling about eating, excreting, washing, dressing, or
> undressing. Such a toddler grows up to be an obsessional dawdler
> about play, chores, and studies.[3]

Furthermore, "teachers-to-be" learned the unproven notion that
without attacking the causes of neuroses true changes in behavior
cannot occur, and even if symptoms alone are rectified, other more
serious symptoms may develop (Kubie, 1958).

> Consequently, unless these earlier neurotic deviations have
> been effectively resolved in the home before the youngster
> reaches school, they will invade and warp his later approach to
> study of all kinds.[4]

A presumably logical extension of untested, and in some instances
untestable, hypotheses derived from psychoanalytical theory have
been reflected in practices that teachers have been advised against
using by some members of the mental health professions. The
teachers have been warned to:

1. not use intrinsic rewards for purposes of motivation because
   these somehow encourage undesirable attitudes.
2. not demand higher academic performance until the *emotional blocks* have been resolved since one must be *cured*
   before he can learn.
3. not provide highly structured classroom settings because
   children will be unable to act out their frustrations.
4. not use aversive techniques or withhold pleasure when
   reacting to misbehavior because children may feel rejected.

Teachers, in programs of preparation, have been exposed to principles of learning that are derived from other theories. Often in the
past, these were presented in such a manner that little direct application to classroom activities could be made. The principles were
often derived from studies with animals as subjects. Those studies
that used humans were generally attempts to study learning principles. In recent years however, there has been a noticeable shift
toward studies of human behavior (Staats, 1964).

Most successful teachers probably stumble upon and use, in an
unsystematic fashion, portions of reinforcement theory. They soon
learn that extrinsic rewards are sometimes necessary and that with-

---

[3] L. S. Kubie, *Neurotic Distortion of the Creative Process* (Lawrence, Kansas:
University of Kansas Press, 1958), p. 117.
[4] *Ibid.*, p. 117

holding rewards is at times necessary in order to maintain classroom control. Until recently teachers have been unprepared to utilize basic principles of learning in a systematic way, therefore many are unable to teach disruptive children effectively.

The discussion that follows is an attempt to present for teachers some principles that can be used when teaching children with learning and behavioral handicaps. The total concept is called **directive teaching.**

Directive teaching of children with learning and behavioral handicaps has three basic propositions, namely that:

1. learning is reflected in a change in behavior,
2. complex forms of human functioning are learned, and
3. because behavior is learned it can be changed.

With the above assumptions in mind, this chapter is devoted to a discussion of how behavior and learning are interrelated. Following a discussion of rewards, some principles of reinforcement will be explained.

LEARNING AND BEHAVIOR: INTERRELATED

Something must happen in order for learning to occur. In other words, without some type of behavior little learning will take place in schools. Behavior in some form is required of learners, and if teachers are engaged in activities for which they were employed, teacher behavior should serve to expedite learning.

Teachers may *lecture* and if children *listen* some learning could take place, or children may be instructed to *write* a word, that was newly introduced to them, ten times in succession as a method of learning to spell that word. A student who *reads* for pleasure can strengthen his reading skills and also gain an appreciation for reading as a form of entertainment. Behavior need not be evident. *Thinking* for example results in learning although one can only infer that it occurred.

Teacher Behavior

Children learn outside the confines of school and without teachers present. Sometimes they learn in spite of teachers, but the most effective academic learning takes place when teachers work in harmony with students.

Importance of Pleasant Teachers / A harmonious teacher-pupil relationship can result in a well-managed classroom environment and efficient instruction. Teachers who are viewed as pleasant by their pupils can pair good feelings that students associate with being in their classes with tasks that are perceived as less pleasant by the pupils. By associating a pleasant event with an activity that has a neutral value, students begin to place a positive value on the neutral event. Through this process, called pairing, it is possible to develop attitudes toward school tasks that were originally not greatly valued.

Each of us has our individual style of building rapport with pupils. Getting to know each pupil as a person is probably the first step toward a positive relationship. A brief interview with each pupil before a crisis arises and before the school year gets well underway can serve as a starting point. The teacher should find some attribute of the student that deserves recognition and compliment him for possessing it. The meeting can be used by the teacher to let the pupil express his likes and dislikes concerning school, whereupon the teacher can support his right to dislike certain school activities and also indicate to the student that most people have preferences. In order to be pleasant, the teacher should avoid arguing with the pupil or lecturing him on the importance of school activities.

As a result of the interview the teacher will acquire clues concerning the student's attitude toward teachers and school. The teacher will also be in a better position to initiate activities that the student dislikes so that he will make an attempt at doing undesirable but necessary tasks.

Teachers as Models / Teachers often serve as models for many children. They emulate their teachers' mannerisms, attitudes and expressions. The concept of modeling is meaningful for those students who are greatly influenced by their teachers.

A student who imitates any aspect of his teacher's behavior is receptive to being influenced by that teacher's actions. Even if the student's imitative behavior is negative, that is if he mimics derisively, it should be noted that he observed his teacher and was influenced by the behavior.

Students tend to identify with, and may imitate, individuals whom they aspire to be like. Consequently, teachers who are respected by their students and who are viewed as capable human beings will probably serve as models for many children with learning and behavioral handicaps.

Teachers transmit other less obvious attributes to students. Their attitude towards other people is conveyed by the manner in which they address others and refer to them in the presence of students. Some teachers ridicule others, are tough and insensitive, and assume they teach subject matter instead of children. Those teachers provide models that may encourage youngsters to replicate the teachers' behavior. But teachers who are warm, who believe that children are more important than subject matter also provide models that may influence student behavior. The admired teacher's attitude toward subject matter is also frequently assimilated by students. Children who identify with their teachers assume many characteristics that were learned through observations of their teachers. When teachers show excitement for their instruction, they stimulate student interest and convey their own interests to students, while a lack of teacher interest will do little to encourage students in attempting to learn.

Teachers as Managers / Classroom management has long been recognized by teachers as an important function. Particularly in special programs for children with learning and behavioral handicaps, skillful management is valuable because often a highly structured school environment is required where teachers must plan each segment of their day. Some of these children are readily affected by excessive stimuli, making it necessary for their classrooms to be tightly organized so that they can focus on essential features in the learning environment.

Managerial aspects of teaching are becoming even more important with the rapid increase in computer-assisted instruction and other mechanisms for individual attention. Such devices require competencies beyond those of typical teachers, since knowledge of prepared programs and awareness of methods for establishing instructional outcomes become elements of classroom management. When teachers separate the outcome of their instruction from its content, they perceive learning as more than acquiring information.

By specifying desired results beforehand, teachers establish a basis for selecting the content to be used. For example, if it has been determined by her teacher that Joan should learn to divide by tens, Joan should be provided with the necessary instruction and material to achieve that outcome (to divide by tens).

Note that establishment of specific goals results in ordering teacher behavior as well as student behavior. Teachers can readily know when a change in student behavior is indicated by specifying outcomes in advance of instruction. When students achieve desired results, teachers can observe their terminal behavior. In this instance, the desired terminal behavior is to divide by tens. When Joan successfully meets the required outcome, her teacher can specify another goal in arithmetic.

Student Behavior

An earlier statement indicated that learning results in a change in behavior. Learning is, in addition, a process that occurs as a result of student behavior. A child who memorizes spellings of selected words is engaging in a behavior (memorization) in order to achieve an outcome (spell words). And because he can now spell a particular word, he can behave in a new way.

Children also learn the particular responses that constitute a behavior. The child was taught to study the spelling of words through rote memory. Even though this behavior is less efficient, and requires more time than other methods of study, he persists in approaching word study in this fashion because he has received some measure of success through the use of memorization. Since learning occurs when the act that is performed is reinforced or rewarded he will continue to study words through this method because his success, small as it may be, has reinforced his behavior. In order for him to change his study habits in spelling, it will be necessary for other approaches (behavior) to be tried. And it will be necessary for him to gain success (reward) with these different approaches.

Attitudes are also learned through behavior. Students who are successful in school related activities usually have positive feelings toward academic pursuits. They enjoy school and look forward to learning. They associate feelings of success with school and willingly put forth additional effort when necessary in order to be even more successful. Students who experience frequent failures in activities associated with school tend to became discouraged and show little persistence when faced with school tasks.

Changing Behavior

Teachers are confronted with problems in getting children to substitute new behaviors for older, more established ones. If the teacher sought to change the aforementioned child's method of learning to spell words by teaching him to use principles of syllabication in conjunction with memorization, it would be necessary to:

1. teach rules of syllabication to the child,

2. show him how the rules can be applied to spelling,
3. get him to use syllabication when learning to spell words, and
4. reinforce his behavior when he uses the new approach.

Other kinds of behavior are also learned. Classroom behaviors, like study habits, are attained often indirectly. Young children acquire classroom routines by obeying their teachers' commands:

> *Please raise your hands.*
> *Please wait until I call your name before answering.*
> *Don't interrupt while others are talking, please.*

They also learn through observing actions of others. Youngsters who transfer from another school at mid-year typically assimilate routines of their new group in a short time by watching the behavior of their classmates.

Learning Inappropriate Behavior

Just as children learn behavior that enhances their adjustment, they sometimes learn inappropriate behavior because it is unintentionally reinforced.

> John learned to get his teacher's attention by throwing scraps of paper on the floor. Miss Johnson, his first grade teacher, saw John inadvertently drop paper on the floor one day. She asked John to pick up the paper. Since John rarely got such individual attention, he began to throw paper on the floor when he was desirous of Miss Johnson's attention. John trained his teacher well for she frequently gave him attention when he engaged in wrong behavior.

Similarly, the "class clown" engages in attention getting schemes because it is his way of gaining recognition. He learned that by acting in such a manner as to elicit laughter from his peers the attention of the class would focus on him.

Relationship of Reinforcement to Learning

E. L. Thorndike's law of effect (1927) advances the notion that any behavior that results in satisfaction to the individual is more likely to be learned. Responses that are used in securing satisfaction become fixated and are learned. As the student utilizes a similar response to a given stimulus and receives satisfaction, reinforcement occurs. If the response is not rewarded, there is less likelihood that it will reoccur when the learner is faced with the same stimulus.

Nature of Rewards

When a response is followed by an event that results in a reduction of need, the event is termed a "reward" which is used here synonymously with positive reinforcement.

Negative reinforcement, which is not emphasized in this text, is a response to a behavior that is dissatisfying to the learner. Punishment and other forms of aversive techniques constitute negative reinforcers.[5]

For purposes of our discussion, rewards, or positive reinforcement, are classified into three groups: 1) primitive rewards, 2) interim rewards, and 3) social rewards.

Edibles that are used as reinforcers constitute primitive rewards. Food has long been used to shape behavior particularly among animals in experimental settings. It is also used to domestic pets. Food is so widely known as a reward that it is used by parents as a means of encouraging similar behavior. It is also used to discourage behavior when it is withheld from children who misbehave and when they are sent to bed without dinner.

Candy and other edibles have been issued to human subjects in association with or immediately following a desired response. The literature is replete with reports describing the management, treatment, and education of children with learning and behavioral handicaps through the use of food.

Care should be exercised when using food stuffs as rewards for at least three reasons. First, their ease of issuance can result in over-rewarding and students will quickly be satiated, causing the edibles to lose their effectiveness. Even if one is careful not to over reward, the tangible nature of edibles is such that other adults will be quick to issue these to the same children without understanding the principles of reinforcement. Satiation could be the result. Second, ingredients of certain foods, particularly sweets, may be harmful to some children. Those who are diabetic should, of course, avoid sweets, and glucose, one form of which is commonly used in sweets, greatly contributes to tooth decay. Three, primitive rewards are several steps removed from the socializing influence that is desired

---

[5] I believe positive reinforcement to be more useful to teachers than negative reinforcement. The latter is not viewed here as inherently bad, although it is often misused by some teachers.

and expected within a school setting. The ultimate purpose of reinforcement is to build in motivation for desirable performances. Other types of rewards are closer to this goal than are edibles and are more naturally a part of the school environment.

School personnel are advised to exercise certain precautions when using foods and objects in school settings. Make certain that the desired responses cannot be obtained through the use of higher order reinforcers, interim or social. If it is determined that it is essential that primitive rewards be issued, these should be paired in association with social or interim reinforcers. These can then become secondary rewards while gradually phasing out the primitive reinforcer. Individuals who issue primitive rewards should carefully emphasize the student's response in order to focus on the behavior instead of the reward.

Parents shoud be notified prior to the use of consumables and objects. Certain toys and objects may be objectionable to some parents (Bijou and Sturges, 1959). Further, parents should be advised not to give these tangibles to their children at home as a matter of course, since to do so may serve to weaken their effects. A sound rule is to avoid using primitive rewards in school except when desired responses are not obtainable through the use of higher order rewards.

Interim Rewards / A stimulus that has come to be associated with a conditioned response will tend to reinforce behavior. The sight of a cone of ice cream, to a child who likes such goodies, will be associated with a desire for ice cream. At another level, the letters ICE CREAM will trigger off similar desires in children who associate the configurations with that frozen delicacy. Auditorily, the sound ICE CREAM will also arouse positive feelings.

When a stimulus is presented repeatedly in the presence of a positive reinforcer, it tends to acquire the force of the positive reinforcer (Sluckin and Slazen, 1961). If a primitive reward is paired with an unconditioned stimulus that is social in nature (such as a smile), the social stimulus will acquire the properties of the primitive reinforcer. The social stimulus can then be substituted for the primitive reward and it becomes a secondary reinforcer.

The term *interim rewards* is used here as a way to designate symbols and objects that come to represent something of value to an individual. School marks and other symbols of academic progress such as stars and displays of student accomplishments are classifiable as interim rewards. Money and other tokens probably represent the most common form of this type of reward.

Interim rewards are useful with learning and behavioral handicapped children because they provide, as the phrase suggests, a bridge to other less tangible reinforcers. These are particularly valuable in the technique of pairing which is discussed in this chapter and throughout other portions of this book.

FIGURE 3.1. A SCHEDULE FOR PAIRING INTERIM REWARD WITH POTENTIAL REWARD

Schedule	Interim Reward	Potential Reward
1 _ _ _ _ _	*	o
2 _ _ _ _ _	*	o
3 _ _ _ _ _	*	o
4 _ _ _ _ _		o
5 _ _ _ _ _	*	o
6 _ _ _ _ _		o
7 _ _ _ _ _		o

Figure 3-1 shows a schedule that can be used to develop additional rewards by using an interim reward in association with a neutral event or stimulus (potential reward). Similarly, a pairing technique can be used to produce new rewards by using primitive or social rewards in conjunction with an existing reward.

The schedule of pairing can vary. In figure 3.1, pairing occurs through three consecutive responses and the potential reward is used alone with the fourth, sixth and seventh responses. If the students continued to emit desired responses using only the potential reward, it would become a actual reward and could then be used in association with other potential rewards. Following the sixth or seventh response, if students do not display desired responses, pairing can again be implemented for more response intervals prior to issuing the potential reward alone. Such a pairing schedule can be used with as many responses as desired.

The issuance of prizes and other objects occurs on occasion in schools. It is an accepted fact that the effects of such rewards tend to encourage the recipients to continue in their winning ways and serve as incentives for others. These are interim type rewards since they serve to bestow social recognition (social reward) upon the recipients. Often circumstances surrounding awarding the prizes, such as the social setting and applause, are more rewarding than the prizes.

Social Rewards / Typically, school age children have become responsive to many secondary rewards through experiences. Often those stimuli that have acquired the attributes of reinforcers are social rewards. Praise, a smile, peer approval, physical proximity, encouragement, and recognition are among the stimuli that have been used as social reinforcers. Any reinforcement that is secondary and not tangible and that considers opinions and attitudes of others as important meets the definition of a social reward.

Use of Rewards

Teachers have access to a wide variety of reinforcers. *Attention* is a powerful reinforcer for many children. If a child gets attention for a certain act (response) he is likely to want to do it again. *Approval,* such as a pat on the back, nod of the head, saying "good" or "that's right," is a common reinforcer. Activities within the school program, such as recess and art, can serve as rewards for desirable performance. Other frequently used rewards are privileges, desired seating arrangements, additional time for enjoyable activities, and desired classroom duties. A number of factors should be considered in order to use rewards wisely.

Selection of Rewards / Rewards must be considered of value to learners if they are to be effective. Until the stimulus is viewed as reinforcing by the student it will have little effect on his responses. Youngsters who do not value school marks will be unwilling to perform if these are the only incentives that are held out as rewards.

Teachers that believe some children are unmotivated are probably overlooking at least two facts about reinforcement. First, they have failed to understand that students are moved by reinforcers other than those used by the teachers. Second, responses expected of these children must be within their repertoires. That is they must possess the prerequisites for responding in the desired manner.

Rewards not only vary with individuals, they are also related to time and task. At a given time, or in a given setting, a reward may be less or more desirable to a particular student. In some instances, children find praise reinforcing but not under other conditions. For example, in the presence of peers, some children may be embarrassed by praise from teachers but not from other students. Others would find praise rewarding from either peers or teachers.

Task requirements may dictate what is reinforcing to a student. A smile may be sufficient for reinforcing a child's participation in group discussion, but it may be viewed as insufficient for demands expected of the same child in completing a difficult and time consuming arithmetic assignment.

The person who issues rewards is also a variable to be considered. A disliked teacher who provides a smile as a reward is probably viewed differently than a well-liked one who provides a smile for the same behavior.

It should be clear from this brief discussion that teachers must have knowledge of other factors concerning reinforcement in addition to the reward preference of a given student. They must know under which conditions students prefer specific rewards for a particular task.

Social Rewards / Teachers should begin with social rewards when initiating reinforcement procedures with a child for the first time. If social rewards are effective, they will have avoided difficulties caused by moving children from primitive rewards toward interim and social rewards. If these rewards are insufficient to influence their responses, then lower level rewards should be used.

New Rewards / Additional reinforcers can be developed through a procedure of pairing rewards with events (potential rewards). A frequent use of pairing contributes to creating many new reinforcers that can be used when needed. The process involves the systematic application of a reward for desired responses in association with a potential reward (see figure 3.1). By associating the two, the power of the first tends to transfer to the second, thus eventually creating an additional reward. The following illustration shows the use of pairing.

> Jasper responds positively to a soft pat on the back from his teacher but is oblivious to verbal compliments from afar. His teacher decided to pair a pat on the back (reward) with verbal compliments (potential reward). She began by approaching Jasper, patting him on the back and voicing approval for his good behavior. After having used the above procedure several times, she asked Jasper to come to her whereupon she complimented him for his desirable conduct and patted him on the back. After having used this second approach four times, she began to alternate it with the earlier procedure. Soon she was able to praise Jasper from afar without the use of other reinforcement. It resulted in a more convenient way of managing Jasper in the classroom.

Internal Reinforcement / Instruction is effective when students find sufficient satisfactions in learning with a minimum of obvious reinforcement. When this occurs, rewards are internalized by the learners.

Other sources of internal reinforcement are found in a particular assignment or task that students enjoy, or in especially attractive instructional material that is rewarding to its users. Individuals who cannot account for reinforcement as a means of motivating students are searching for solely external rewards. They are ignoring the intrinsic rewards which may be contributing to the children's desirable responses.

Teachers should also recognize that some students persist in repeating easy tasks because ease and resulting feelings of success are internally rewarding. As task demands are increased, however, as is often the case when teaching new skills or concepts, internal rewards are no longer sufficient and more obvious external rewards are needed. In other words, when teaching children with learning and behavioral handicaps we should view those who do not need obvious reinforcement as not engaging in new learning because the present task demands are too easy.

Timing of Rewards / Reinforcement, to be effective, should occur simultaneous with the desired response or should immediately follow it. For this reason, school marks as typically used in report cards have little reinforcement value since reports to parents seldom occur frequently enough to be reinforcing.

When a child gives a correct response, his answer should be quickly reinforced if the teacher wishes to establish a connection between the stimulus and the response.

Frequency of Rewards / If a response is conditioned and is then reinforced less and less frequently, it will have greater lasting power and be more resistent to extinction. Initially, when establishing a connection between a stimulus and a response, frequent rewarding is often necessary. As the response becomes conditioned, however, reinforcement should not be presented everytime.

> After getting Jasper to respond to praise, his teacher gradually reduced the frequency of the reward. Because he could not anticipate when praise would be forthcoming, Jasper behaved in a praiseworthy way for longer and larger periods of time.

Schedules of Reinforcement

Planned reinforcement requires an established schedule that can be followed by teachers in the classroom. Two general schedules of reinforcement are commonly used. These are: 1) continuous schedules and 2) intermittent schedules. Figure 3.2 shows a comparison of these two schedules of reinforcement.

FIGURE 3.2. A COMPARISON OF CONTINUOUS AND INTERMITTENT
SCHEDULES OF REINFORCEMENT

Schedules Responses	Continuous Reward	Intermittent Reward
1	X	X
2	X	X
3	X	
4	X	X
5	X	X
6	X	
7	X	X
8	X	X
9	X	
10	X	X

Differences between continuous schedules and intermittent ones are exemplified in figure 3.2. Reinforcement is provided after every response on a continuous schedule, while reinforcement under an intermittent schedule does not occur after every response. The intermittent schedule in figure 3.2 is designed to issue rewards to success responses with no reinforcement every third response. Both of these schedules are fixed types because the rate of reinforcement does not vary.

Continuous reinforcement is used when a reward is presented every time a desired response is given. After a response is established, the schedule should be changed so that reinforcement is not presented every time the desired response takes place. When this change is made, the schedule is then termed intermittent and it results in more stable behavior. Four types of intermittent schedules are described below:

1. Fixed-Interval Schedules: Once a response is established (which may require immediate reinforcement of every response) we can then reinforce it at certain clock intervals, every five minutes or every hour. Although the response rate becomes slower, the response is more stable and more immune to extinction, but another process sometimes intervenes. Immediately after reinforcement, the response rate may become lowered since no reinforcer is immediately forthcoming.

2. Variable-Interval Schedules: A low probability of response due to reinforcement on a fixed-interval schedule can be eliminated by using variable-interval reinforcement. Instead of reinforcing a response every ten minutes, we can vary it so that it is now one minute, now thirty minutes, etc., but averages every ten minutes. Using this type of schedule results in a response that is very difficult to extinguish.

3. Fixed-Ratio Schedules: Under fixed-ratio schedules reinforcement occurs every X number of responses. This is a quite inefficient schedule, for it results in long pauses between reinforcements, especially if the ratio of responses to reinforcement is high. To avoid long pauses after reinforcement, a schedule similar to a variable-interval one can be introduced.

4. Variable-Ratio Schedules: Variable-ratio schedules are highly efficient and hard to extinguish and produce high rates of responses. Under this schedule we may reinforce every second response at one time, and every 80th response at another time. The student has no way of anticipating when a response will be rewarded and therefore takes no chances.

Note that intervals refer to *time* while ratios are used to designate *number*. Consequently, certain behaviors are more easily responded to on a time basis while others lend themselves to use with frequency of occurrence. Figure 3.3 shows a comparison of a fixed schedule with a variable schedule of reinforcement.

Other Conditioning Approaches

The preceding discussion in this chapter was concerned with techniques that are based upon the stimulus-response model. It views learning as resulting from connections between situations (S) and responses (R). Thus, a child who replies to a given stimulus must gain satisfaction from his response in order for him to engage in similar behavior when again confronted with that situation.

Other conditioning approaches have great promise for use with children who have learning and behavioral problems. These include:

1. operant conditioning,
2. contingency management, and
3. behavioral modeling.

FIGURE 3.3. A COMPARISON OF TWO INTERMITTENT SCHEDULES OF
REINFORCEMENT: FIXED-RATIO AND VARIABLE-RATIO

Schedules Responses	Fixed-Ratio Reward	Variable-Ratio Reward
1	X	X
2	X	
3		X
4	X	X
5	X	
6		
7	X	X
8	X	
9		X
10	X	X
11	X	X

It can be seen in Figure 3.3 that a variable rate does not permit the subject to know when rewards will be issued while the fixed schedule is easily anticipated.

Operant Conditioning

Up to this point we have discussed behavior that is elicited by presenting stimuli. What if desired behavior already occurs from time to time without any particular pattern? If we wish to further develop the response so that it is emitted more often or at more predictable times, operant conditioning techniques could be applied (Skinner, 1938).

Probably the most widely known conditioning approach is that of operant conditioning (Reynolds, 1968). Operant behavior is behavior that operates on the environment. An operant is not a single particular response but rather a class of responses that are likely to occur. The responses are conditioned or made to occur more frequently or more strongly by reinforcing desired behavior.

Operant conditioning permits teachers to take advantage of children's responses. Let us say that a teacher is faced with a student who is a disruptive influence in the classroom. Through observation, the teacher determines that praise for good behavior is seen by the child as rewarding. When he is behaving appropriately, the teacher takes advantage of the desired behavior by reinforcing it with praise. By reinforcing any behavior that approximates the one that is wanted, it is possible to establish new operant behavior. Initially, it is sometimes necessary to reinforce any behavior that exists and then gradually begin to reinforce those responses that are in the desired direction.

Few people achieve perfection when learning a new skill, concept, or task. Rather, learning occurs through a series of steps, one built upon another. Using the notion of approximating a desired result, teachers should break instruction down into minute steps and reward each correct response. By teaching in this fashion, they will be calling for an approximation of an assignment and reinforcing each attempt in the proper direction. As the student succeeds and develops that response, the teacher can build upon prior successes and request an even closer approximation of the assigned task.

Let us suppose that Joan's teacher wanted her to learn skills needed for mastery of spelling words. The teacher noted that Joan responds favorably to verbal praise. Her teacher asked Joan to write the ten words that were assigned that week. She praises Joan for copying all ten words correctly. Joan is then told to study three of the words by dividing each into syllables and writing each word as she pronounces the word aloud. She is asked to repeat the process ten times for each word.

After completion of the aforementioned assignment, Joan's spelling of the three words is tested. She spells the three words correctly and is praised for her success.

The process is repeated. Each time more words are added. After each trial test, Joan is praised for her efforts and her successes. Gradually, through a process called *successive approximations* Joan's performance is equivalent to that expected: the mastery of ten spelling words for that week.

Contingency Management

Teachers often tell children that after they have performed a certain task in a specified manner they may have a reward. Teachers who use the "first do this, then you get that" approach state that the reward is contingent upon a desired behavior.

In order for contingency management to be effective, teachers must be aware of the students' desires in relation to the required tasks. In other words, pay off for children's performances must be of sufficient value to them so as to guarantee their attempts.

Rewards in school typically may include special privileges, selection of preferred activities, special recognition, and favorable school marks. Teachers can use charts in conjunction with contingency management. Under this plan a master chart is displayed in the classroom. As students complete an assigned task, it is recorded on the chart. When a given amount of points are accumulated, students may select their reward, or teachers may announce in advance of the assigned tasks that students will be rewarded for good performance.

> John, after you have finished this arithmetic assignment, if the problems are done correctly, you may go to the library corner and select a book.

Presumably, in the above example, the teacher has established that John has difficulty in the completion of his arithmetic and that the privilege of selecting a library book is viewed by John as rewarding.

Behavioral Modeling

Earlier it was indicated that children learn through observing others. Bandura (1962) has demonstrated that social learning occurs through imitation and that children readily copy the behavior of those who provide attention as reinforcement.

Children, furthermore, tend to model their behavior after that viewed on film as well as real behavior. Because of prior real-life experiences and vicarious experiences enjoyed by children through movies and television viewing, they come to school with a variety of already established imitative behavior.

Rewards can be effective reinforcers with modeling techniques in at least two general ways:

1. by issuing reinforcers to children who copy desired behavior and
2. by providing vicarious reinforcement to children who model their behavior appropriately.

The first, giving reinforcement for desired behavior, can be depicted as follows:

> Students in Mary's reading group are praised loudly by the teacher for quietly completing their workbook assignment, a task that Harold's group seldom does quietly. The teacher rewards

(praise) Mary's group so that members in Harold's group can hear.

She then turns to Harold's group and requests that they do their workbook assignment in a quiet manner. After the group did what was requested, they too were praised for their desirable performances.

The second method of reinforcing, through vicarious means, permits using several media. Teachers can tell or read stories, assign readings, use film, and display pictures that depict people receiving social approbation or other forms of reinforcement for desired behavior. Without actually giving an external reinforcer, one can reinforce certain performances by exposing students to examples of behavior and by informing them of the results of their performances.

Miss Smith wishes to teach a group of disruptive students to be more cooperative and sensitive toward each other. She tells them a story about a group of children who were faced with a series of challenges that required patience and cooperation from the entire group. Descriptions of social interactions within the fictionalized group are clearly presented. As a result of the cooperation, the group in the story emerges successful.

The secondary reward of success is used in the above account as a means of teaching that group cooperation pays off.

Many successful teachers have used reinforcement approaches without necessarily being aware of the importance of a systematic application. As we become more conscious of our own behavior as well as student behavior, we will be more effective in teaching children with learning and behavioral handicaps.

Summary

Psychoanalytical psychology and its derivatives have had an inordinate influence upon teacher attitude. Assumptions upon which such theories are based have little applicability to problems of teaching.

Principles that recognize learning as a form of behavior and permit teachers to function as behavioral specialists are derived from reinforcement theory.

Reinforcement is used to develop desired behavior. It is classified into three groups: primitive, interim, and social. The use of rewards involves careful selection of reinforcement, an emphasis on secondary type rewards, and the development of new rewards through associative techniques.

Timing of rewards and the frequency of their issuance are of primary importance. Schedules of reinforcement are based on continuous and intermittent patterns with the latter preferred.

Other conditioning approaches are operant conditioning, behavioral modeling, and contingency management.

Gathering
Descriptive
Information

Effective teaching takes place when ⸻ **FOUR**
classroom activities are clearly related to
specified outcomes. By establishing what will constitute desired
results in advance of instruction, teachers have a basis for selecting
appropriate instructional materials and for deciding which strategies to use in order to achieve specified outcomes. In order to
establish specific instructional objectives, it is necessary to acquire
behavioral information that is instructionally relevant. This chapter
contains descriptions of procedures for acquiring relevant information.

At least four types of information about students are relevant for
teaching. These are:

1. *Academic Skills:* Teachers must know which skills children have yet to master, have already mastered, and are in
   the process of mastering.

2. *Sensory Channels:* Teachers should know which sensory
   channels are most effective for their students to receive the
   needed instruction.

3. *Behavior:* Teachers need information concerning conditions in school under which their students emit desirable
   and undesirable behavior.

4. *Reinforcement:* Teachers need to know which events are viewed by their students as rewarding when learning academic skills and behavioral responses.

Teachers have been advised for years to begin teaching "where the child is" but seldom have they been informed as to how one determines the specific point at which to begin instruction. There are probably many reasons for this gap between advice and practice. Among these is the lack of availability of the pertinent information needed by teachers. Information, to be helpful for teaching, should consist of specific descriptions of current educational behavior. When teachers specify what children know, are unsure of, or do not know, they can identify where to start teaching. After determining what reinforces students for given tasks or activities, teachers have the necessary ingredients for devising teaching plans.

Sources of this information are typically within the school. If they are not present, however, procedures can be established by teachers along with other school related personnel, such as psychologists and counselors, to acquire relevant information. Most schools have testing programs in which standardized tests of achievement and intelligence are administered to students routinely. The test results are often recorded and filed along with other information about the child in a cumulative record.

Ferguson (1963) has noted that the primary purpose of cumulative school records is to serve as a resource for school personnel so that they can devise an effective educational program for each pupil. Cumulative school records of children who exhibit problems are frequently chronicles of school difficulties. Because special education teachers typically face these children after they have been in the general school program and after they have been evaluated by a host of specialists, cumulative folders should be sources of important information. Sometimes they contain clues that can help teachers decide upon those instructional approaches most suitable for teaching each child.

It is a sound practice to analyze the students' folders carefully prior to testing or seeking information from additional sources. Teachers will find it necessary to extract information, as well as to reinterpret data, since records are designed and kept for many different purposes. The use of a summary form by teachers will help them to synthesize bits of information that are behaviorally relevant and valuable for instructional purposes because such information in many instances will be scattered throughout the cumulative folder. If the summary form is carefully designed, completion of it will serve to sort out those items that are needed and directly relate to teaching.

Only a portion of school records are sufficiently current to be of immediate value for teaching. After extracting what relevant information does exist in school records, additional knowledge of educational functioning will be needed. The discussion that follows describes an assessment process to be used by teachers, school psychologists, and other educational personnel who are responsible for gathering instructionally relevant information for use in directive teaching.

ASSESSMENT OF FUNCTIONING

Assessment, as used here, is a survey of student functioning. Its purpose is to determine those responses and skills which are adequate and those which need to be taught or improved. The term *assessment* is used to convey a meaning more specific than "testing." It is distinct from diagnosis which means to identify a disease or abnormality after studying its origin. Educational diagnosis results in classifying students on the basis of educationally relevant information (English and English, 1958, p. 150).[1] Labeling students' problems (diagnosis) and classifying students (educational diagnosis) are not considered to be instructionally valuable.

Implementation of directive teaching is based upon current knowledge of students' academic achievement, behavior, and reward systems. Assessment of these three functions can be accomplished through formal or informal means. The former is represented by standardized tests and inventories while the latter category is composed of teacher observations, teacher-made tests, and interviews.

It is assumed that physiological examinations and, when necessary, medical treatments were provided prior to those assessments that are discussed below. However, such examinations and treatments are not necessary preconditions for the assessment of learning problems and, in fact, are often the results of teacher observations. Referrals to medical practitioners are frequently made by school

---

[1] It is noteworthy that "assessment" is rarely defined in other than economic terms, such as assessment of property. When found in literature it is often used synonymously with the term "measurement."

officials when physiological factors are believed to be contributing to learning failures.

Assessment of Academic Achievement

Information concerning academic performance must be highly specific if it is to be helpful for teaching. Knowledge of school achievement is typically obtained from either or both of two sources:

1. standardized tests that are designed to measure school achievement and

2. teacher-devised tests that are usually given to students prior to and following a period of instruction.

When tests are administered prior to instruction and following instruction, they can serve both as measures of learning and as indicators of what should be retaught.

Observable aspects of academic performance are classified under two categories: academic skill areas and sensory-expressive modes. These categories are discussed below.

Academic Skills

It is necessary either to develop tests of school achievement that isolate skills and principles that children know and do not know, or to adapt presently available tests for use in assessment since teachers need much more detailed information about students' academic skills than is yielded by such tests.

Uses of standardized tests / Grade scores, commonly obtained from standardized achievement tests, are useful when comparing a student's position to a reference group but are too gross and consequently have limited instructional value for teachers. It is not enough for a teacher to know that a student is reading at the third grade six month level (3.6) or that his word recognition exceeds his reading comprehension. While a reading grade score suggests an approximate grade level for selection of instructional material, it tells teachers little about:

1. specific reading skills children have mastered and those they have yet to learn,
2. children's understanding of what they read, and
3. words they recognize and those they do not know.

Assessment of academic skill functioning can be accomplished by using tests as types of observations. Those tests mentioned here have been used for such purposes and are merely presented as examples of a wide selection of available materials. Furthermore, these may not have been developed for use as depicted here. The test authors might have devised these instruments for use as predictors of adjustment or for determining diagnoses, but they have

FIGURE 4.1.   SAMPLE ITEMS FROM THE DIAGNOSTIC ANALYSIS OF LEARNING DIFFICULTIES CALIFORNIA ACHIEVEMENT TESTS LOWER PRIMARY BATTERY[2]

1. Reading Vocabulary

A. *Word Form*

☐ 1, 3, 4 — Identical words, lower case

☐ 2, 7, 12, 16, 17, 21, 24, 25 — Different words, lower case

☐ 14, 19, 23 — Different words, capitals

☐ 6, 8, 9, 11, 13, 15, 22 — Identical words, mixed forms

☐ 20 — Different words, mixed forms

☐ 5, 10, 18 — Reversed words

B. *Word Recognition*

☐ 1, 11 — Gross differences

☐ 2, 3, 5, 7, 9, 12, 13, 18 — Final sounds

☐ 4, 6, 10, 16, 17 — Initial sounds

☐ 8, 14, 15, 19, 20 — Middle sounds

C. *Meaning of Opposites*

☐ 1-15 — Basic vocabulary

D. *Picture Association*

☐ 1-9 — Identification of objects

☐ 10-15 — Location of objects

Test of Letter Recognition

☐ 1, 2, 3, 4, 5, 6] Lower case

☐ 7, 8, 9, 10, 11, 12] Capitals

☐ 13-24 — Mixed forms

3. Arithmetic Reasoning

A. *Meanings*

☐ 1, 2, 3 — Picture-symbol association

☐ 4, 5, 6, 7, 8, 9] Recognizing numbers

☐ 10, 11, 16, 17, 18, 19] Writing numbers

☐ 12, 20 — Sequence of numbers

☐ 13, 14, 15 — Comparison of numbers

☐ 21, 22, 23 — Value of coins

☐ 24, 25 — Telling time

☐ 26, 27, 28 — Weight & time concepts

☐ 29, 30 — Symbols & abbreviations

B. *Problems*

☐ 1, 2, 3, 6, 8, 10, 11, 12, 15] One-step problems

☐ 4, 7, 14 — Budgeting

☐ 5 — Sharing

☐ 4, 5, 7, 9, 13, 14] Two-step problems

D. *Subtraction*

☐ 1-15 — Number facts

☐ 1, 3, 5 — Subtracting zeros

☐ 16-20 — Two-place simple subtraction

☐ 20 — Borrowing

5. Mechanics of English

A. *Capitalization*

☐ 1, 2, 8, 14 — Names of persons or animals

☐ 3, 11, 16, 19,] Pronoun "I"

☐ 4, 5, 17, 20 — First words of sentences

☐ 6, 7, 9, 12, 18] Names of months or days

☐ 10, 13, 15 — Names of cities

B. *Punctuation*

☐ 1, 3, 5, 8, 9, 15, 17, 20] Periods

☐ 2, 4, 7, 10, 12, 14, 19] Question marks

☐ 6, 11, 13, 16, 18] Commas

C. *Word Usage*

☐ 1, 4, 8, 11, 14, 25] Number

☐ 2, 3, 9, 10, 12, 19, 23, 24] Tense

been found to be useful when gathering relevant instructional information.

Standardized achievement tests are commonly used to determine achievement level, but can also be used for analyzing learning difficulties. One such test is:

California Achievement Tests, by Ernest W. Tiegs and Willis W. Clark (Monterey, California: California Test Bureau, 1957).

The complete battery measures skills in Reading, Arithmetic, and Language at the lower primary level (Grades 1 and 2). It can be given to large groups of children at one time and it yields grade scores in each skill area. Of more importance to teachers is the fact that it also has an easy format for analyzing each student's specific strengths and weaknesses. Figure 4.1 shows a form that accompanies the California Achievement Tests, Lower Primary Battery.

We can conclude from an analysis of her performance on the reading portion of the Wide Range Achievement Test that Joan:

–did not readily recognize the twelve words shown in Figure 4.2,
–had difficulty attacking words of more than two syllables,
–had difficulty determining which syllables should receive the accent.

FIGURE 4.2.   ERRORS MADE BY JOAN ON READING SECTION OF
WIDE RANGE ACHIEVEMENT TEST[3]

Word as Shown	Word as Read
aboard	a broad
rancid	run side
bibliography	bib lee graf e
unanimous	u na mouse
scald	scold
mosaic	moss ik
predatory	per date re
municipal	mun a pole
decisive	dis a viv
contemptuous	cont emp tess
deteriorate	det or ate
stratagem	stra tag um

[3] J. F. Jastak, S. W. Bijou, and S. R. Jastak, *Wide Range Achievement Test* (Wilmington, Del.: Guidance Associates, 1965), used with permission.

Joan's performance on the Arithmetic Computation Section of the WRAT resulted in an arithmetic grade score of 4.2. An analysis of her calculations reveals that:

- she added whole numbers correctly including three column addition, indicating that she carried correctly in addition.
- she did not add fractions with common denominators correctly ($1/3 + 1/3 = 2/6$).
- she subtracted problems not requiring regrouping accurately ($5 - 3$; $4 - 1$; $29 - 18$).
- she failed to calculate correctly one problem ($\$62.04 - \$5.30$) that required regrouping.
- a problem in division [$6\overline{)968}$] requiring carrying was incorrectly answered.
- she failed to answer correctly a question concerning the amount of minutes in 1½ hours.

Specific information can be obtained from any achievement test. In order to use tests in this way, teachers must know the sequence of skills so that they can select items to be taught that are not only incorrect but do not require prerequisites that students have yet to learn.

There are also commercially available achievement tests that are designed for assessment purposes. These usually require special training and time to administer. While most teachers can readily learn to use these instruments, the amount of time required for a complete assessment often prevents their use. An ideal arrangement is for teachers of children with learning problems to have ready access to the services of a psychometrist or a psychologist who can conduct testing and provide teachers with results. Because of limited availability of these services, many teachers will find that using less detailed and less time consuming tests, like the WRAT, is more practical. When time and circumstances permit, a comprehensive test of academic skills is preferred.

Skills within a subject area can also be assessed through inventories that can be administered to groups. Often these are developed to accompany textbooks. An example is:

The McKee Inventory of Phonetic Skill by Paul G. McKee (Boston: Houghton Mifflin Company, n.d.).

This inventory was initially developed to accompany the McKee Reading for Meaning Series. It can be used to determine which phonetic skills a child knows or does not know irrespective of the reading series used. It is divided into sections, each of which taps a particular phonetic skill. Figure 4.3 contains a part of the section that tests knowledge of vowel sounds.

FIGURE 4.3. SAMPLE ITEMS FROM MCKEE INVENTORY OF PHONETIC SKILL TEST THREE [4]

ripe	rip	reap	rope	rap	fall	fowl	foil	file	foal
lean	lone	loon	lane	loin	bit	boot	bout	bait	beet
spoke	spike	speck	spake	spook	sun	sin	sine	sown	sane
hay	haw	hoe	he	hew	mud	mode	mood	maid	mid
meal	male	mill	mole	mull	crack	creek	croak	crook	crock
pen	pine	pain	pawn	pun	did	dude	dud	deed	dead
sick	sock	sack	soak	seek	rid	reed	rod	rude	raid
ten	tan	tone	tin	tine	flew	flaw	flow	flay	flee
peach	pouch	pitch	poach	pooch	pay	pow	pew	paw	pea
shine	shin	shun	shone	sheen	low	law	lee	lie	lo
meat	mote	mutt	mute	mate	tail	tile	toil	tool	teal
sir	sire	soar	sour	sear	stall	style	steel	stale	stole
pile	pill	pale	pal	peel	oil	awl	eel	ill	ail

The *Kindergarten Evaluation of Learning Potential*[5] is designed to assess children of kindergarten age, although it can be used with older children who are achieving at or below a pre-first grade level. The KELP provides for evaluating performances on eleven items: skipping, color identification, bead design, block design, bolt board, calendar, numbers, safety signs, writing a name, auditory perception, and social interaction.

The KELP test materials are intended to be used for evaluation as well as for teaching. Experienced teachers of young children will find the KELP easy to administer. Suggestions for teaching each item as indicated in the manual should enable even beginning teachers to use the materials effectively.

Teacher-devised achievement inventories / It has already been indicated that teachers may conduct analyses of learning problems at varying levels of depth. Subtest scores can be compared for general purposes. Similar test items can be categorized, at another level, to show areas of weaknesses and strengths. More specifically,

---

[4] Paul G. McKee, *The McKee Inventory of Phonetic Skill* (Boston: Houghton Mifflin Company, n.d.), used with permission.

[5] John Wilson and Mildred Robeck, *Kindergarten Evaluation of Learning Potential* (KELP) (New York: Webster Division, McGraw-Hill Book Company, 1965).

each test item can be examined to determine students' instructional needs in a given skill area. Finally, if desired, an analysis of one academic skill can be accomplished.

Perhaps a teacher-devised achievement inventory can best be used for attaining the last two purposes, namely: 1) to survey academic skills of students and 2) to analyze students' mastery of specific academic skills.

The first purpose can be accomplished by using informal testing techniques.[6] One procedure for assessing reading achievement is to have the student read aloud a section of graded material with a series of increasingly more difficult levels (Betts, 1957). As the student reads, note words mispronounced. Following the reading, ask the student questions to assess reading comprehension.

Informal assessment of silent reading comprehension follows a similar procedure. It is recommended that the survey be preceded by a test of word recognition, such as the reading section of the Wide Range Achievement Test. With an estimate of the student's level of word recognition, teachers will have a basis for determining where silent reading should begin. A sound rule to follow is to start with material that is approximately two years below the student's word recognition level, giving him early success with the reading material and continuing to a point where the reading matter cannot be comprehended by the student.

The teacher should select a graded series of paragraphs and instruct the child to read each paragraph silently indicating that questions will be asked about what was read. While the student reads the teacher should observe to see if lip movements and other signs of poor reading occur. When observing the child's performance, the teacher should determine the level at which all questions were correctly answered, evidence of tensions, and where all words were recognized. This is his independent reading level. It is at this level that students can be expected to read without teacher assistance.

The instructional reading level has been described by Otto and McMenemy (1966, p. 124) as the level where some teacher supervision is needed. These authors suggest that comprehension at this level should be at least 70 percent with about 95 percent accuracy in word recognition.

Informal assessment procedures are also useful when estimating

[6]For other informal techniques, see J. W. Birch, *Retrieving the Retarded Reader* (Indianapolis: The Bobbs-Merrill Co., Inc., 1955).

students' applications of principles of syllabication. For example, a series of words that are consistent with principles of syllabication can be used to determine if students apply these principles. The following consists of words that relate to the four vowel principles that students are typically taught to apply in fourth grade:

Principle 1

In words or syllables containing only one vowel, the vowel is usually short unless it comes at the end of the word or syllable. i.e., *short* in: pan, shut, mat, and mit, *long* in: go, tiger.

Words in List:

ban	bat	bad	bag	can
nap	pad	yap	jag	tan

Principle 2

In words or syllables containing two vowels, one of which is final *e*, the first vowel is usually long and the final *e* is silent, i.e., wise, gate, amuse.

Words in List:

trade	grape	vase	bathe	shave
grave	mate	skate	dame	fake

Principle 3

When two vowels come together the first vowel is usually long and the second one is silent, i.e., meet, scream, hoe, oak, main.

Words in List:

bead	tea	cheat	flea	preach
leak	heath	leash	cheap	yeast
day				

Principle 4

In words or syllables containing only one vowel followed by *r*, the sound of the vowel is usually governed by the *r*, i.e., curl, jar, carpet.

Words in List:

star	far	tar	car	mat	curt

Principle 5

In words or syllables containing only one vowel and followed by *l* or *w*, the sound of *a* is usually governed by the *l* or *w*, i.e., claw, halt, awful, almost.

Words in List:

malt	ball	calk	dawn

The above vowel principles are surveyed by the following word list:

ban	trade	bead	star	nap
shave	bat	preach	curt	malt
dawn	pad	dame	yap	cheap
bad	grape	tea	far	ball
jag	calk	grave	leak	tar
dawn	tan	fake	yeast	car
cheat	bag	vase	heath	flea
mar	mate	day	leash	curt

This list of words is presented and the student is asked to read each word aloud. The teacher notes words that are mispronounced. These are then related to the list containing vowel principles as a means of quickly determining those that the child does not use.

Similar techniques can be used to assess other academic skills. For example, a general test of arithmetic fundamentals can be administered that surveys skills over a range from simple to complex.

An analysis of pupils' mastery of a particular skill can be accomplished through informal means by presenting items that are a part of one process, such as division, to determine which features of the process are not accurately performed. The pupil can also be asked to describe the process he used so as to determine where he went awry (i.e., "Work the problem aloud for me." or "Find the sentence in the story that proves your answer.").

Summarizing information[7] / It is helpful for teachers to have a form for summarizing information about students' academic skills particularly since such information may be obtained from various sources. The following academic skills summary form shows information about Joan's computational skills in arithmetic.

---

[7] I wish to acknowledge the aid of Mr. Harold Chew in recognizing such a need and for his helpful suggestions concerning summary sheets.

Academic Skills Summary

Student: Joan   Subject: Arithmetic

Skills needing to be retaught	Dates of Observations
Division, carrying	9/15
Division of two or more place numbers	9/14

Skills needing careful introduction and teaching	
Minutes in an hour and half hour	9/15
Addition of common fractions	9/15
Regrouping in subtraction	9/15

The format, as shown above, provides spaces for noting new skills to be taught and those skills to be retaught. By indicating dates of observations, teachers have a record of when the need for the skill instruction was discovered.

Receptive-Expressive Modes

Learning is dependent upon an individual's capacity to assimilate sensations from the environment. The use of such information is evidence of learning. Explanations of this process involve the reception of information by the human organism, the integration of information, and responses (Osgood, 1957).

The following diagram is based on Osgood's model of human communications.[8]

Receptive	Integrative	Expressive
visual	order	speaking
auditory	storage	hearing
haptics	association	moving
olfactory		smelling
		touching

Receptive and expressive modes are observable and are relevant to this volume. However, the integrative process is based on hypo-

---

[8] I wish to acknowledge many helpful conversations with Professor G. D. Stevens about the process of receiving and using information.

thetical considerations and biological explanations concerning neural pathways and thought processes which are presumed or covert and will not be discussed further.

Receptive Modes

The human organism has several receptive channels through which sensations are received. These receptor systems serve to provide learners with information. Intact auditory, visual, haptics, and olfactory functions are essential for learning. Children who do not receive high quality auditory or visual signals are likely to be seriously handicapped and are designated as deaf or blind. Our discussion is not concerned with those who are so profoundly affected but rather with children who have difficulties in discriminating and recalling stimuli through any sensory channel. In these instances, the level of acuity is sufficient for receiving stimuli but the discrimination and recall through any of the channels are defective resulting in disturbed or hampered signals.

Teachers can make accurate decisions concerning instruction when they have knowledge about learner characteristics. Knowledge of how a student learns includes knowing which receptive channels are operative for a given type of stimulus and knowing which receptors are less effective for receiving similar stimuli.

The emphasis here is on evaluating students' effectiveness in learning subject matter through each modality and on improving achievement in academic skill areas. The purpose is not to test sensory modalities and to then train students in an attempt to improve sensory learning isolated from academic achievement.

Expressive Modes

The expressive behavior of students is important to teachers because responses suggest what students have learned. Results of learning are observed in students by their actions or responses to stimuli. These actions may take the form of moving, speaking, smelling, and touching.

We can determine if stimuli have been received by students through their reactions to signals. If John is asked to erase the chalkboard and he responds accordingly, we can assume from our observations that he received the auditory signal. Similarly, if the signal is given in written form John's behavior will indicate the extent to which he follows, as well as receives, the visual stimulus.

John's teacher, Mr. Smith, wrote the following on the chalkboard: "John, please erase this chalkboard." Mr. Smith asked John (an auditory signal) to follow the instructions as shown on the board. John looked at the sentence but then sharpened a pencil and began writing at his desk. Based on the observed behavior, Mr. Smith can assume that John either did not receive the signal or refused to follow it.

His failure to receive the signal could be due to his inability to see the sentence, possibly he was too far from the chalkboard, or his reading skills may be inadequate and he could not decode the message. John also may have received the signal but ignored it. Any of these possibilities can be tested by Mr. Smith. Conditions can then be changed so that John will appropriately respond to visual stimuli.

The assessment techniques discussed in this chapter will help determine if students are responsive to various sensory stimuli. These techniques can be used by teachers without special training.

Assessment of Expressive Modes

A distinction should be made between assessing learning processes and assessing expressions of learning. Results of assessing learning processes are viewed as aptitudes and are commonly associated with tests of intelligence that are then used to predict achievement.

Test items that purportedly measure memory span, for example, include digits or words that are presented aurally. Results of a student's performance on such items may be used as clues by a psychologist to suggest ways in which the student may learn effectively or poorly. Thus, good performance on tests requiring memory for aural material may indicate that the student has good facility to learn aurally. We would expect a positive, but far from perfect, correlation between a score on a test that measures auditory aptitude with an achievement test score. To some degree, the two performances are related. We should expect a closer relationship, however, between measures of aptitude in subject matter, such as arithmetic, and with achievement in that subject. Even with this more direct application the correlation will not be perfect.

Assessment of expressions of learning is necessary for measuring achievement, but the purpose is not to apply the findings to an ability criterion as with results from intelligence testing. Rather, it is to determine if the student expresses academic content that presumably was assimilated through certain sensory channels.

Expression is defined here as any observable response. Expressions are rarely unitary; they often involve several modalities in consort rather than singularly. In assessment, however, it is helpful to isolate individual modes of expression because the purity of the response under testing conditions will suggest the extent to which that particular sensory channel can be used for learning. There is merit also in combining sensory modes when testing in an effort to assess the additive strength or weakness that results when learning activities rely heavily on two or more modalities. Instructionally relevant information about expressions of learning should be clearly related to skill areas that are defective. A child, for example, with a problem of reading should be assessed with reading material. It is insufficient to assume that similar processes are involved in recognizing, for instance, differences among geometric designs when in fact poor achievement is noted in a failure to discriminate words.

The examples that follow describe informal ways of measuring expressions by isolation of one sense and a brief discussion about the combination of two or more senses.

Assessment of Visual Learning

Assessment of what is learned through vision involves visual discrimination and recall. Discrimination as used here means the detection of differences in sensory processes (English and English, 1958, p. 156).

Visual discrimination / In order for effective learning to take place through sight, accurate discrimination of visual stimuli is necessary. Serious problems of visual discrimination among school age children are characterized by difficulty in differentiating likenesses and differences between objects and/or printed symbols and failure to distinguish figures from backgrounds.

When problems of visual discrimination exist, careful observations of students' performances will reveal clues that can be used for teaching. Learners who display difficulty in differentiating visual differences among words but who discriminate words auditorily may profit from instruction that relies more heavily upon hearing than seeing. Furthermore thorough instruction in visual discrimination of words may result in improved reading performance.

A systematic observational method for determining accuracy of visual discrimination involves selecting visual material from an academic skill area in which the student has manifested difficulty. Set a criterion level below which discrimination will be deemed inadequate by stating in advance of testing the percent of correct responses acceptable for passing. When establishing a criterion level, remember that the test items should be compatible with the child's age and academic achievement, and that test reliability increases with additional test trials. If the test material is selected so as to represent easy and hard levels of difficulty and if each set of material is within the same subject area, successes on each succeeding trial should not greatly exceed those on earlier trials.

After setting a criterion level, items are presented to the student to test accuracy of visual discrimination. Such activities will vary, depending upon the nature of the material and its level of difficulty. The student is then asked to repeat those items that were incorrect. If necessary, errors made by him should be pointed out to him.

Instructional material, to which prior exposure has not occurred, should be selected and the student's visual discrimination should again be tested. A check on his errors should be made by asking him to repeat the items that he missed.

While assessing, the examiner should note the child's performance on the known material as compared with his responses to the unknown material. Discrepancy between trials may have significance for subsequent teaching. If greater success was evidenced on the first trial (known material) than on the second trial (unknown material) it is reasonable to assume that visual discrimination is adequate for learning that type of task and that additional exposure and instruction will result in more success in learning the difficult material. If serious errors are noted in both trials, one should assume that visual discrimination is inadequate with this type of task.

Assessment of visual discrimination can be summarized as follows:

1. Select visual stimuli from an academic skill area in which the student has difficulty.
2. Set a criterion level below which visual discrimination will be considered inadequate.
3. Assign exercises to the student that will test accuracy of visual discrimination. These will vary depending upon the nature of the material and its level of difficulty.
4. Ask the student to repeat those items that were incorrectly seen and, if he repeats the errors, tell him the correct responses.
5. Select instructional material to which he has not had prior exposure.
6. Again, test his discrimination.

7.   Ask him to repeat the items missed.

Example: Joan's discrimination of reading matter was tested in the following fashion:

She was asked to read the 220 basic sight words that comprise the Dolch vocabulary list (Dolch, 1936). Because of her prior school experience, there was good reason to expect that she had had prior exposure to these words in reading materials. Errors made by Joan that suggest inadequacies in visual discrimination are shown below. The correct words are in parenthesis:

made (make)	you (your)	want (went)
there (where)	will (well)	went (want)

When these words were called to her attention Joan read each word correctly.

Discrimination of more difficult words also appeared to be inadequate. Figure 4.2 on page 66 shows errors made on the reading section of the Wide Range Achievement Test (WRAT). Errors that suggest problems are seen in:

aboard (abroad)	scold (scald)
rancid (run side)	predatory (per date re)

Similar testing in arithmetic (reading number symbols aloud) did not reveal any errors.

We can conclude from the analysis of visual discrimination in reading that Joan's performance does indicate minor difficulty but it probably can be overcome by calling to her attention details in word formations.

Visual memory / Visual discrimination may be accurate but memory of what is seen may be inadequate. In such instances, teaching through the vision chanel may require modification of instruction or less reliance on that sensory mode. Thus, if the child's visual discrimination is accurate but his recall of symbols that were experienced visually is poor, the teacher may still wish to emphasize vision as a major mode for learning but will build into the instruction mnemonic clues.

Memory can be categorized along a temporal dimension that includes immediate recall and delayed recall. These two types of recall will be discussed in that order.

immediate recall. Procedures for assessing immediate recall of visual stimuli are:

1.   Select material that consists of known symbols or forms.
2.   Present selected material to the child and tell him to look

carefully at the selection because it will be removed and he will be asked to identify it from among other materials.

3. After a pre-arranged time interval remove the material and present another set of material containing similar items with the previous material embedded. Have the subject select those items that were shown to him on the first showing.

4. Repeated trials with equivalent materials should be conducted to ascertain that chance factors did not contribute greatly to the selections.

The preceding steps are exemplified below by referring to an assessment of immediate recall of spelling words with Joan. The testing material was used following the administration of a short test in spelling in which she misspelled the words *correct, circle, suggestion,* and *halo.*

Example:

Examiner: Joan, I am going to show you a card with four words on it. Look carefully at the spelling of each word because after five seconds I am going to take the card away and show you another one with the same words on it spelled differently. You will be asked to select those words that are spelled correctly.

Card One:

      correct   circle   suggestion   halo

Examiner: (After 5 seconds) Now look at these words, point to the ones that are spelled the very same way as they were on the first card.

Card Two:

corect	cerrect	correct	carrect
circle	sercle	cercle	sircle
sugestion	suggestion	seggestion	siggistion
halow	helo	hallo	halo

Examiner: Point to the word in the first line that you saw on the first card. (After the child points, record his response and proceed to the next line using the same format.)

delayed recall. One of the most emphasized demands in schools is to demonstrate accuracy in recalling material. Consequently, failure in such activities handicaps students severely in school.

Memory over time is dependent upon such factors as the effectiveness of initial learning, the meaningfulness of instruction to the learner, and the effects of distractions caused by similar instruction during the interval between teaching and recalling. Irrespective of which factors influence delayed recall, knowledge of a student's performance will be helpful to his teacher.

Procedures used in assessing delayed recall of visual material follow the sequence used to assess immediate recall except that the elasped time between cards one and two is considerably greater. Further differences occur if the child is taught material and then examined at a subsequent point. For example if following the spelling test, the spelling errors had been pointed out to Joan, noting the correct spellings as shown on card one, card two could have been shown to her the next day in order to test delayed recall of material that was taught solely through a visual approach.

The results of measuring recall of visual material can indicate how much reliance should be placed on memory when instruction is based on a visual approach. If the student demonstrates adequate discrimination but poor immediate and delayed recall of visual material the teacher would want to use other sensory clues to support visual instruction, or overlearning may be used to improve recall. When immediate recall is good but delayed recall is less than adequate, short periods of instruction well spaced over a long segment of time may prove effective in teaching the student to retain visual material over time.

Assessment of Auditory Learning

Language is learned chiefly through the auditory channel and, because higher orders of thinking are dependent upon language symbols, deafness is considered to be a debilitating handicap. Problems of auditory learning can be present even when hearing acuity is within the normal range. These difficulties include: a) auditory discrimination and b) recall of auditorily received stimuli. Both are discussed below.

Auditory discrimination / Auditory discrimination involves the extent to which sounds are distinguished from other sounds. The relevance of such discrimination to speaking and reading is great because those sounds that are imprecisely heard are not learned correctly.

Auditory discrimination can be assessed as follows:

1. Select material that is within the examinee's listening comprehension.
2. Set a criterion level below which performance is inadequate.
3. Pronounce the material one unit at a time, tell him to repeat exactly what you say.
4. Note inaccuracies in pronunciation.

Difficulties in auditory discrimination are reflected in mispronunciations of common words and the confusion of similar sounds. Children who demonstrate weaknesses in this area may profit from hearing training. In addition, the teacher should use multi-sensory aids whenever possible in order to offset the auditory deficits.

Auditory memory / Recall of auditory stimuli should also be assessed on a delayed and immediate memory basis. The procedure for measurement is similar to that of assessing other sensory recall. Every attempt should be made to have the student use only the sensory channel that is being evaluated.

  immediate recall. Each step for assessing immediate recall of auditorily presented material is indicated below followed by an example.

  1. Select material that is within the listening comprehension of the student and set a criterion level.

  Example:
  Joan is reading on a beginning fourth grade level. Therefore, select a short segment from easy third grade reading material. By choosing a selection that is below reading comprehension level, there is reasonable assurance that it will be well within her listening comprehension level. A criterion of 100 percent was set.

  2. Tell the student to listen carefully while you read aloud because when you are finished you will ask questions about the story.

  Example:
  "Katy was a little elephant. She lived in a big jungle. She lived with many other elephants. The elephants ate grass and leaves from trees."

  3. Ask questions about the material.
  "Who was Katy?"
  "Where did she live?"
  "What did the elephants eat?"

  4. Record the number of successes and failures.

Joan correctly answered the three questions and met the criterion of 100 percent.

  delayed recall. Recall of auditory stimuli that were presented at any earlier time can be evaluated similarly using the following procedures:

1. Select material that is within the listening comprehension of the student and read the material to him. Follow the directions in number two above.

Example:

Joan's immediate recall of the previous selection proved to be good. She answered each of the three questions correctly. Because of her success with that story, she demonstrated that it was within her listening comprehension. Consequently, that same selection and, in fact, the same reading of the story can be used to assess her delayed recall of auditory stimuli.

2. After 24 hours or more have elapsed, ask questions about the material.

Example:

Teacher: Joan, yesterday, I read a story to you about Katy. See how many of the same questions you can answer today.

	"Who was Katy?"
Joan:	"An Elephant.'
	"Where did she live?"
Joan:	"In the jungle."
	"What did the elephants eat?"
Joan:	"Hay"

Joan answered two out of three questions from a listening exercise that was delayed 24 hours. We can rate her delayed listening comprehension of auditory stimuli to be about 66 percent (⅔ of the responses were correct). If we use a criterion of 100 percent (3 correct answers out of 3 questions), Joan's delayed recall of detail was not acceptable.

Results from assessment of auditory learning will suggest the emphasis that should be placed upon the auditory channel and the extent to which a heavy reliance on this channel detracts from learning. Remedial teaching may be directed toward emphasis on improving the weaknesses in the auditory discrimination of the subject matter found in the assessment. While the teacher may avoid the auditory channel when presenting difficult or new material, easy material may be used to improve auditory learning. In the latter instance, a channel that does discriminate well should be used in conjunction with the weaker one. For example, material requiring the use of visual discrimination as well as auditory discrimination should be used if one channel is more effective in learning than the other.

Assessment of Haptic Processes

The importance of the sense of touch for teaching some children with learning problems has been demonstrated by Fernald (1943). She described how memory of form is sometimes facilitated when the input is through the sense of touch in combination with other sensory avenues. Children learn through the sense of touch when they perceive objects hapticly.

Haptics is the sense of touch in its broadest sense (English and English, 1958, p. 236). Informal ways of assessing discrimination and recall of haptic stimuli are described below.

Haptic discrimination / The effectiveness of learning hapticly can be assessed by closing off the other sensory channels during the assessment process.

1. Select educationally relevant material that is within the demonstrated achievement level of the child.

Example:

Materials used to test Joan's haptic discrimination are: a ball point pen; a wooden cube; an egg shaped stone; a key; and cardboard forms of a triangle, a diamond and the letters T, P, O, and Q.

2. With the test materials hidden, the student is blindfolded and given one object at a time to feel. He should try to identify each object.[9]

3. Each response should be recorded.

Example:
Joan's responses are shown below preceded by the stimulus items:

Stimulus	*Response*
ball point pen	a pen
egg shaped stone	a stone (Teacher: Yes, but what shape is it?) Round.
cube	a square
key	key
triangle	triangle
diamond	another triangle

The following were presented by placing Joan's hand on the form without removal of the items from the table. By using this procedure, the teacher prevented confusion due to changes in position.

---

[9] It may be necessary to begin with the child closing his eyes and not blindfolded if he is unduly fearful.

Stimulus	*Response*
T	T
P	P
O	O
Q	Q

Two of Joan's answers were incorrect, the egg shaped stone and the diamond. All others were correct. Her haptic learning appears to be good, at least with the stimulus items that were used. Because of her success in haptic discrimination, a more difficult task was used in assessing memory.

Haptic Memory / Memory can be tested with information obtained from assessing students' haptic sense.

immediate recall. The purpose of measuring immediate recall of haptic stimuli is to determine if that sense serves as a channel for learning. Suggested procedures for assessment follow.

1. Select material that has not yet been mastered by the child but is near mastery.

Example:
   Joan, on a spelling test, misspelled these words as shown: corect (correct); heven (heaven); beleve (believe). It is reasonable to teach Joan how to spell these words since the errors she made in an attempt to spell them suggest that they approach accuracy.

2. Teach the child the material through heavy reliance on haptics.

Example:
   Joan was asked to trace with her finger the manuscript form of the words three times.

3. Test the child, upon completion of the special instruction, in order to assess the effects of practice through the haptic sense.

Example:
   Joan was asked to spell the words that she had just traced. Her performance is shown below:
   correct (correct)   heven (heaven)
   beleve (believe)

The added practice only resulted in Joan's learning to spell one of the three words (correct).

delayed recall. The effects of stimuli that are received hapticly can also be measured over time. The procedure is similar to that used in assessing immediate recall except number three occurs at a later point in time. If the student has demonstrated success on the immediate recall testing, the procedure in number four below can follow in 24 hours or more to determine if the learning was maintained.

4. Retest using the same material that was taught at least 24 hours before.

Example:
The next day following assessing immediate recall, Joan was asked to spell the words she had traced. The teacher provided the auditory stimulus (pronounced the word) and Joan wrote her response. All three words including the word "correct," were misspelled.

It appears that while her haptic discrimination seems adequate, Joan did not demonstrate that haptics is a channel through which difficult words are learned.

Assessment of Olfactory Learning

Olfactory learning is used here to mean the extent to which one distinguishes odors and associates smells with known objects. We learn to associate odors with many stimuli. Although we are aware of odors and their influence on human behavior, little has been written that is directly concerned with olfaction in learning. Schachtel (1959, p. 298) accounts for our negligence of the use of smelling as a channel for teaching because of a cultural taboo. Consequently, it has been relegated to an indirect means of learning and it is seldom used by teachers in a conscious, orderly way.

Olfactory discrimination / The recognition of odors and the differentiation of one fragrance from others comprise what is meant here by olfactory discrimination. Steps for testing olfactory discrimination are:

1. Select at least three distinctly different odors.

Example:
Using identical size blotting paper, soak in odoriferous fluids for an equal amount of time. Use two pieces of blotting paper for each odor. Number the papers serially and record those numbers that represent matching odors.

2. Present the odors to the subject, restrict the use of other senses.

Example:
Tell the subject to match those papers that smell the same.
Note in this example, there is no need to blindfold the subject
since the pieces of blotting paper do not provide other sensory
clues.

3. Record the number of pairs that were correctly matched.

We can also measure the recognition of known objects through
olfaction simultaneous with a test of memory.

Memory of olfactory stimuli / The purposes for assessment of olfactory memory is to determine if the subject uses odor as a means of
identifying stimuli and as a way to recall previously experienced
stimuli. An assessment process follows:

1. Blindfold the child and tell him that you have a number of
   objects for him to smell.
2. Present a stimulus; do not permit him to hold or to examine
   the objects tactually.
3. Ask him to smell the stimulus and to name it; record his
   responses.[10]
4. Repeat the cycle using those items that were missed by the
   subject. Tell him the name of the object as he smells it.
5. Repeat the cycle, asking him to identify all the objects
   again. Proceed as described in steps one and two.

Example:
Examiner. I have five things in separate bags here. After you
are blindfolded, I'll put one object at a time under your nose and
tell you to smell it. But you can't hold it. Tell me what it smells
like.

Five objects are presented; a piece of chocolate candy; cinnamon; slice of orange; slice of onion; and a banana. A criterion
score of 3 was set. Joan earned a score of 3, recognizing all but
the cinnamon and the banana.

Because Joan met the criterion score, it was unnecessary to test
her olfactory recall. Evidently, her delayed recall for these odors is
good since she recognized them on the first trial, demonstrating that
olfaction is a sensory mode that can be used in teaching Joan names
of objects can be taught in conjunction with their odors.

Perhaps the facility to distinguish and recall smells has more
potential when attempting to change behavior. Suggestions in this

---

[10] Upon the completion of this step, if the examinee meets the criterion level,
recall through olfactory cues is demonstrated. If criterion was not met, proceed
with the next steps.

Figure 4.4. SENSORY-EXPRESSIVE LEARNING SUMMARY FORM

Student's Name   Joan

Dates of Assessment   September 9, 10

Sense Skill	Stimulus	Criterion Score	Performance Score	Analysis Code (○, at criterion; — below; +above)	Comments
AUDITORY					
Discrimination	20 pairs of words — subject to indicate same or different	18	18	○	answered 18 of 20 correctly; failed sit-set; knit; net
Immediate Recall	Story: "Katy"	3	3	○	answered 3 of 3 questions
Delayed Recall	Same	3	3	○	
VISUAL					
Discrimination	220 Dolch Words	220	214	—	word recognition improves when detail is called to her attention
Immediate Recall	word selection — 4 trials	2	3	+	recognized correct, circle, halo; missed suggestion
Delayed Recall	word selection — 4 trials	3	4	+	recognized all 4 including suggestion
HAPTIC	objects				geometric designs recognized
Discrimination	letters	8	9	+	letters T, P, O, Q, recognized
Immediate Recall	Spelling words: correct, heaven, believe	3	1	—	recalled "correct"
Delayed Recall	Same	1	0	—	failed all 3 words
OLFACTORY					
Discrimination	Chocolate candy, cinnamon, orange, onion, banana	3	3	○	missed cinnamon, banana; at criterion
Immediate Recall					
Delayed Recall	Same	3	3	○	at criterion

regard are provided in the sections that deal more specifically with social behavior.

Analysis of Expressive Learning

The preceding discussion, concerning assessment of sensory-expressive learning, described procedures that were intended to limit the use of sensory receptors in order to evaluate the effectiveness of a single expressive mode. An analysis should be conducted of the student's expressive learning after the sensory modalities have been assessed. A view of results in juxtaposition provides the teacher or the examiner with a quick comparison of the child's assets and liabilities in the sensory-expressive learning area. Figure 4.4 shows a format that is used for summarizing these results. It contains a profile of the expressive learning assessment of Joan.

The summary of Joan's sensory-expressive learning suggests that:
–her best discrimination appears to be in haptics; olfactory and auditory discrimination is adequate; but visual discrimination is below criterion level.
–recall seems best with visual learning and poorest in recall of haptic learning; delayed recall of materials presented hapticly is below criterion.
vision, a primary mode for learning, appears to be Joan's weakest area for initial learning.

Implications for teaching / Even though visual discrimination is below criterion, Joan's recall of material that has been experienced visually is good once it is learned. The problem appears to be one of making sure her visual discriminations are accurate. Conversely,

Stimulus	*Choices shown to Joan*						
battle	pr	b	l	v	d	br	p
break	pr	b	l	v	d	br	v
prattle	pr	b	pl	v	d	p	bl
plow	pr	b	pl	v	d	p	bl
peek	pr	b	pl	v	d	p	bl
blow	st	b	pl	v	d	p	bl
vat	st	b	pl	v	d	p	bl
bat	st	b	pl	v	d	p	bl
struck	st	b	pl	v	d	p	bl

auditory discrimination of words is good but recall is somewhat less than adequate. In this instance, teaching Joan word recognition by using auditory cues should result in mastering learning tasks that require visual discrimination. The following procedures reflect a combination of auditory and visual discrimination.

Words were presented to Joan both visually and auditorily; each word was pronounced by the teacher as it was presented visually. Joan was asked to select the initial sound of the word as represented visually.

Observation of Learning

It may not always be feasible to conduct careful assessments of each student's expressive modes. When time is limited or when ancillary services are not available, a skillful observer can acquire considerable information about the learning styles of children through less detailed assessments. However, teachers who do conduct careful assessment on individual children will be more adept at spotting defects in learning of other children. When teachers must rely on less systematic means of assessment, time may be lost and effort wasted later due to inadequate assessment.

An understanding of the psychological components of learning probably serves to accelerate the remediation of academic skills. This understanding helps teachers to recognize avenues of learning that are most and least receptive to instruction. Such information is sometimes obtained by teachers through observation of students and through teaching trials. The following questions reveal the nature of psychological information that will be helpful to teachers of children with learning difficulties.

1. Motor performance

   How well does he form letters and numbers?
   Does he read and write from left to right?
   Does he write between the printed lines?
   Does he appear to be less well coordinated in gross motor skills than his classmates?
   Does he consistently write with the same hand?

2. Visual discrimination

   How well does he descriminate visual differences in letters, words and numbers?
   How well does he discriminate gross visual differences?

3. Auditory discrimination

Does he accurately repeat sounds, words, and sentences?
Does he accurately pronounce common words?

4. Memory

Does he recall accurately experiences that occurred several
days previously?
Is his recall for immediate experiences accurate?
Does he recall experiences presented in any one sensory
mode with more or less proficiency than that presented in
other modes?

Answers to the foregoing questions provide teachers with clues
to instructional approaches. It should be noted that teachers may
choose to focus on skills that are within weak or strong areas. For
example, a child may have difficulty in auditory discrimination.
Despite this weakness the teacher may choose to emphasize a phonic
approach to word attack skills. In doing so, the teacher may have
selected a task that demands phonetic analysis, or the teacher could
have elected to try to strengthen the student's auditory discrimination. In either event, an evaluation of the instruction will determine
the wisdom of the decision. If the teacher wishes to teach through
an avenue that is defective, frequent positive reinforcement will be
needed. The reinforcement should be presented in small steps so
that gains can be readily made.

Knowledge of children's strong and weak channels of learning
permits teachers to select instructional materials more precisely. If
a teacher wishes to build reading skills rapidly with a child who
discriminates well auditorily but has difficulty in memory, beginning reading material that uses a psycholinguistic approach may be
chosen. If memory is intact but auditory discrimination is poor, with
similar instructional goals, reading material that emphasizes sight
vocabulary would be more appropriate.

Assessment of Behavior

School related behavior is easily identified by the trained observer. Most teachers can, when questioned, describe those characteristics and responses that are emitted by their students. But
without prior training or guidance, teachers have difficulty focusing
on educationally relevant behavior. This is due, in part at least, to

the concept that overt manifestations are symptomatic of unconscious motivations. Irrespective of the motives, if indeed such behavior can be explained in terms of motivation, behavior can be changed more quickly if overt manifestations are the focus of treatment.

Teachers may infer from what is seen without carefully observing all aspects of the behavior. A teacher who is oriented toward *describing* the behavior of a student will readily acquire, through observation, information that is educationally relevant, while one who makes inferences about underlying causes of what is seen will, more often than not, focus on irrelevancies.

Those who receive referrals from teachers for child study services will substantiate the importance of obtaining accurate descriptions of the problem behavior, as opposed to opinions that are based on hypothetical thinking. The reader can test his own predilections toward inferential thinking by reading the statements that follow. Check those conclusions that are based on *observed* behavior, rather than on inferences.

Observation:
1. Mark began annoying Martha during arithmetic instruction. When the teacher asked him to stop talking and pay attention, he shouted obscenities at her.

Conclusion:
a) The level of arithmetic instruction was too difficult.
b) Mark responded vigorously to his teacher's request.
c) Mark is emotionally disturbed and/or brain damage.

Observation:
2. Joan sat all morning with her head on her chest. Even during story time she did not participate in the group discussion.

Conclusion:
a) Joan displayed no involvement in group activities all morning.
b) Joan was daydreaming or was sleepy because she probably went to bed late the night before.
c) Joan is emotionally disturbed.

Observation:
3. Lester began imitating the sound of a pig while the teacher was working with another reading group. All of the children laughed.

Conclusion:
a) Lester was seeking attention.
b) Lester is a very disturbed child.

   c) Lester gained the attention of his classmates.

If you focused on observations, your answers should be: 1) b., 2) a., 3) c. Any other answers suggest that you leap to conclusions that are not based on observed behavior and that you tend to make incorrect inferences.

Types of Behavior Relevant to Teaching

Conditions under which behavior takes place in school must be known in order to affect change. It is insufficient to describe responses without being cognizant of stimuli (reinforcers) that provoke reactions. When it is not evident which stimuli provoke misbehavior, specifying conditions during the interval in which a misbehavior occurs enables teachers to determine when certain strategies should be implemented in order to modify responses.

It is possible to view the types of behavior that are relevant to classroom instruction in several different ways. Verville (1967, pp. 261-264) groups behavioral disturbances among elementary school-age children as "attention-seeking behavior, restlessness, and negativism and disobedience." These three categories probably cover the large majority of disruptive behavior in classrooms. A similar, but not identical, grouping will be used in our discussion with the recognition that the three groups that follow are not mutually exclusive.

Reactions to instruction constitute one general setting in which educationally relevant behavior takes place. Youngsters who have difficulty in attending to instruction are engaging in behavior that interferes with learning. As a result of inattention, their responses are either inappropriate, irrelevant, or insufficient for desirable learning to occur. If children dislike the content being presented and are unwilling to participate as learners, their responses to the instruction will constitute major barriers to learning.

Reactions to others in the learning environment can result in circumstances that diminish learning because of behavior that interferes with learning or that enhances and facilitates learning. Students who respond negatively to teachers' directions, or who engage in hostile acts towards their classmates are thwarting the instructional process. In the latter instance, they may not only be hindering their own learning but they may also be interrupting the learning of others.

Reactions to assignments by students constitute their willingness or unwillingness to engage in independent activities that have been designated as follow-ups to instruction. Assignments in workbooks,

silent reading, arithmetic, and spelling practice all require cooperation from students in order for learning to occur.

Classroom observers may find these categories of in-school behavior helpful as the attempt to specify the circumstances under
which behavioral responses occur.

Methods for Assessing In-School Behavior

Because teachers have many opportunities to observe children
in groups, they can obtain valuable information concerning educational and behavioral functioning of children. If purposes of observations are clearly established in advance, observers will be
prepared to identify pertinent information. An observation form or
inventory will aid observers in meeting the purposes of the observation.

Behavior ratings or check-lists can be used by teachers and others
to assess types of responses that are emitted by students when interacting with others. Such instruments can be devised locally or
purchased from test publishers. Irrespective of the source from
which they are obtained the essential features, for purposes of directive teaching, that should be incorporated into the behavioral
rating devices are:

1. Formats should be relatively simple permitting ease of use.
2. Items to be checked should be observable thus eliminating
   inferential or hypothetical thinking.
3. Items should specify activities and people in the environment with whom the child is interacting.

While external (predictive) validity and reliability are not essential features of instruments to be used for the purposes previously
noted, validity and reliability of the observations are important.
Teachers and other users of instruments should be trained in observational procedures so as to reduce the amount of observer error
due to carelessness and lack of experience in school settings.

Many behavioral rating scales that are available from commercial sources could serve as examples. Only one of these has been
selected for this purpose.[11]

The Child in School by D. H. Stott and Emily G. Sykes[12] contains
about 250 descriptions of behavior. Characteristics of children be-

---

[11] For reviews of rating scales, see O. K. Buros, ed., The Sixth Mental Measurements Yearbook (Highland Park, N. J.: Gryphon Press, 1965).

[12] D. H. Stott and Emily G. Sykes, The Child in School, Bristol Social Adjustment Guides (San Diego: Educational and Industrial Testing Service, 1967).

FIGURE 4.5. SAMPLE ITEMS FROM THE BRISTOL SOCIAL ADJUSTMENT GUIDES, THE CHILD IN SCHOOL

ATTITUDES TOWARDS THE TEACHER

Greeting teacher: Over-eager to greet/greets normally/sometimes eager, sometimes definitely avoids/waits to be noticed before greeting/absolutely never greets/n.n.

Response to greeting: Usually friendly/can be moody or suspicious/mumbles shyly, awkwardly/does not answer/answers politely/n.n.

Helping teacher with jobs: Always willing/very anxious to do jobs/offers except when in a bad mood/never offers but pleased if asked/has no wish to volunteer/n.n.

Answering questions: Always ready to answer/sometimes eager, sometimes doesn't bother/eager except when in one of his moods/gets nervous, blushes, cries when questioned/not shy but unconcerned/n.n.

Asking teacher's help: Always finding excuses for engaging teacher/seeks help only when necessary; seldom needs help/too shy to ask/not shy but never comes for help willingly/too apathetic to bother/sometimes very forward, sometimes pouts/depends on how he feels.

General manner with teacher: Natural, smiles readily/overly-friendly/shy but would like to be friendly/makes no friendly or eager response/sometimes friendly, sometimes in a bad mood/quite cut off from people, you can't get near him as a person/not open or friendly; sometimes 'seems to be watching you to see if you know'/n.n.

Talking with teacher: Normally talkative/forward (opens conversation)/overtalkative (tires with constant chatter)/inclined to be moody/says very little; can't get word out of him/avoids talking (distant, deep)/avoids teacher but talks to other children.

Talks to teacher about own doings, family or possessions — normally for age/excessively/never makes any first approach/chats only when alone with teacher/n.n.

Contacts with teacher: Very anxious to bring/sometimes brings/never brings flowers, gifts, although classmates often do.

tween ages 5 and 16 are categorized as follows: Attitudes Toward
the Teacher; Attitude to School Work; Games and Play; Attitudes
to Other Children; Personal Characteristics; and Physique.

Among the advantages of this check-list is the specific relationship of each item to a behavior, as seen in Figure 4.5.

The Child in School meets the aforementioned four essential features of a behavioral rating. Its format permits easy use; the observer underlines the descriptive phrase that best characterizes the
child. Each item is observable. Each also specifies the activity (i.e.,
"Greeting Teacher") and the person (i.e., "attitudes toward the
teacher") in the environment involved in the interaction with the
child. The instructions for use are clearly shown and can easily be
mastered by the user.

Teachers, school psychologists, counselors, and other school related personnel can devise behavioral observation schedules to serve
the same ends as commercially developed lists. Conditions around
which problem behavior is likely to develop among school age children is shown on a form accompanied by space for the observer to

FIGURE 4.6. OBSERVATION FORM — BEHAVIOR IN SCHOOL

Child _____   Age _____

Date _____

Observer _____   Time of Day: From___to___

Specify the observed behavior. Indicate under reactions: + for
positive, − for negative, and o for neutral. Add notations if
necessary.

1. Reactions to Instruction   Time _____

      Activities   Reactions

               + − o

2. Reactions to Others   Time _____

    Names   Activities   Reactions

3. Reactions to Assignments   Time _____

    Assignments   Reactions

describe the behavior. Figure 4.6 shows such a form following the categories that were discussed earlier.

Behavioral assessment results in an awareness of the *conditions* under which responses occur. Thus when undesirable responses are emitted, baseline information can be obtained that relates to the frequencies of the behaviors and types of responses. The example that follows should serve to clarify the acquisition of baseline information.

> Mark finds it difficult to work independently without becoming disruptive. He begins to talk to others who are nearby and soon he is out of his seat and wandering about the classroom.
>
> He was observed for three days during the times he was assigned workbook activities relating to reading. Mark was clocked during this period and worked at his assignments without disrupting others on the average of 5 minutes. The shortest time interval when he engaged in appropriate behavior was about 3 minutes and the longest was 7 minutes.

The aforementioned baseline information, indicating that Mark maintains desirable behavior for a given time under specified conditions (while doing reading workbook assignments), permits the teacher to anticipate undesirable behavior. Because his teacher knows when to expect such behavior, intervention can occur *before* Mark emits undesirable responses. By reinforcing acceptable behavior, teachers increase the probability of desirable behavior continuing.

Observations sometimes serve to identify stimuli that precipitate unwanted responses.

> Max tends to become violent, striking out at others, when he is ridiculed by other children because of his poor speech.

The teacher has several options available in helping Max control his violent behavior.

1. The teacher can seek to extinguish teasing by Max's peers.
2. Speech correction can be provided.
3. Max can be assisted to recognize baiting and learn to respond in a friendly fashion, thus blunting the stimulus.

Assessment of Reward Systems

A reward system encompasses rewards that are preferred by a student and the necessary rate or schedule for issuing these rewards.

Teachers of children with learning and behavioral handicaps need accurate information about the reward systems of their students. They need to know what reinforcers are effective in strengthening desirable responses from a child. Often it is valuable for teachers to know how frequently responses should be reinforced to insure continuation of the responses.

Seldom is such information available to teachers in a systematic fashion. Nor are observation schedules or inventories readily available for use by teachers in gathering information that is concerned with reward preferences of students.

Techniques to be discussed here for assessing reward systems of students are: 1) observational techniques, 2) interview procedures, 3) forced-choice preference schedule, and 4) the contrived task approach.

Observational Techniques

Teachers, through casual observations, can discover what is viewed as reinforcing to children at a given time. When children ask for storytime or ask when they can play, they have revealed what is rewarding for them at that time. The teacher can then offer these to them as rewards, contingent upon successful completion of an assignment that the children consider to be less desirable.

A teacher who wishes to be more systematic can make note of students' requests and later use these as rewards for desired performances. Such important details as the following should be noted by teachers:

Who prefers to work with whom
Which students like which activities
Which students enjoy attention and from whom
Which students are strongly reinforced by peer recognition
Which students find close physical proximity to the teacher or to others to be reinforcing.

Interview Procedures

Structured interviews can be used to assess what is reinforcing to children. Techniques to be discussed here include those that are designed to be used with an individual child and those that can be used within a group.

Individual interview approach / The teacher should begin with an informal discussion with the child that can serve to establish rapport and that will also provide information. During the interview, the child should be asked to identify which subject he believes is easiest for him and which subject is hardest for him. The teacher should pursue information by seeking answers to additional questions concerning which aspects of a subject are easy or hard.

The exchange that follows between a teacher, who is serving as an interviewer, and 9 year old David will demonstrate phase one.

Teacher: What is the easiest subject for you?

David: Arithmetic

Teacher: What are you studying in arithmetic that you find to be easy?

David: We're learning long division and I like it.

Teacher: What subject do you have the most trouble with, David?

David: Reading and language.

Teacher: What do you find difficult about reading?

David: I have trouble figuring out new words.

The second step in the interview approach is to determine what the child views as rewarding. Potential rewards that are typically used in school with children of this age should be tried initially. The interviewer should describe and, if feasible, show potential rewards to the child, two items at a time.

Teacher: Which of these would make you feel better after you worked on new words in reading?
          1)   a star on your paper, or
          2)   hanging your paper in the room.

David: Put it on the bulletin board.

Teacher: Alright. Would you like that better than putting an A on your paper and sending it home?

David: I'd like both.

Teacher: Of the two, which is better?

David: Putting my paper on the bulletin board.

Had David responded to the question in a manner that was indicative of a lack of interest in either reinforcer, the teacher would have continued offering possibilities until the most preferred reward was identified.

The student is then asked to complete an easy task based on the information provided by him. Upon the successful completion of the assigned task, he should be praised for his accomplishment. Then he should be given a task that he indicated was hard for him. Assist him if necessary. He should be rewarded for his attempts, using the preferred reinforcer. Note his reactions. Figure 4.7 shows the steps used in an interview approach

FIGURE 4.7. PROCEDURES FOR ASSESSING REWARD PREFERENCE: INTER-
VIEW APPROACH

1. Informal discussion with child:

_____easiest subject

_____most difficult subject

2. Ask about two rewards

    a._____

    b._____

3. Ask which is preferred

    Preference_____

4. Remove rejected item, add new reward

    a._____

    b._____

5. Repeat steps 3 and 4 until strongest reward remains.

6. Assign easy task to child.

7. Assign difficult task.

8. Upon completion of 7, administer preferred reward.

Group interview technique / Interviews of groups can be conducted in one setting through the use of paper-pencil inventories. In an oral interview, the teacher asks a series of questions concerning feelings toward school and preferences. As each student responds, answers are recorded by the teacher.

The following depicts a teacher interviewing a group of five boys (ages 8 - 13). Their responses are shown in Figure 4.8.

Teacher:	All of us have things that we enjoy doing in school and things that we would rather not do. Of all the things we do in school, what do you like best, Harry?
Harry:	Recess!
Teacher:	Why do you like recess best of all, Harry?
Harry:	I like to play different games.
Teacher:	Alright, Harry, now of the things we learn in school, what do you like best?
Harry:	I don't like arithmetic!
Teacher:	Why? (The boys begin talking loudly. The teacher lets them continue for a minute and then uses the previously established cue for extinguishing talking out of turn by snapping her fingers and pointing to Harry.)
Harry:	It's too hard. I can't get that regrouping stuff.
Teacher:	Harry likes recess and he doesn't like arithmetic. What do you like to study best of all Mike? (Later she returns to Harry and elicits the feeling that "spelling is alright." Harry gets his best grades in spelling.)

FIGURE 4.8. AN OPEN-ENDED GROUP INTERVIEW: ASSESSMENT OF TASK AND REWARD PREFERENCE

Teacher ___Miss Jackson___ Date ___5/12___

Name	Response
John K.	1. Reading (likes animal stories) 2. Arithmetic and Writing 3. More Storytime
Harry S.	1. Spelling 2. Arithmetic (addition) 3. Recess (use play as a contingency)

FIGURE 4.8. AN OPEN-ENDED GROUP INTERVIEW: ASSESSMENT OF
TASK AND REWARD PREFERENCE (CONTINUED)

Ken M.	1. Nothing 2. Reading and Arithmetic 3. Recess (use play as contingency)
Jack N.	1. Arithmetic 2. Storytime is O.K. 3. Art (like to color)
Mike D.	1. Nothing 2. Everything 3. Likes to Draw (art)

Questions

1. What is the thing you like best to study in school? (If the response is general, ask "What part of that?")
2. What is the thing you like least of all about school? Why?
3. What makes you try hardest when you study?

Forced-Choice Preference Schedule

Interviewing within a group setting sometimes is not feasible for certain age groups and with those students who have strong negative attitudes toward school. Also, teachers should be sensitive to peer pressures that can result in erroneous responses. A paper-pencil, forced-choice preference schedule can be used with students who read. One is shown in Figure 4.9. Because of differences in school programs, the content may need to be changed in order to be useful in other school settings.

FIGURE 4.9. A FORCED-CHOICE PREFERENCE SCHEDULE

Name _____ Date _____

The following numbers should be used to represent the categories as shown:

1 = I like best; 2 = I like; 3 = I like only a little; 4 = I don't like; 5 = I dislike; 6 = I strongly dislike.

Check the activity that you like better between each pair.

1. ____recess
   ____physical education

2. ____reading
   ____recess

3. ____physical education
   ____reading

4. ____arithmetic
   ____reading

5. ____writing
   ____reading

6. ____arithmetic
   ____spelling

7. ____spelling
   ____reading

8. ____spelling
   ____writing

9. ____writing
   ____arithmetic

10. ____ art
    ____music

The results obtained from the forced-choice schedule shown in Figure 4.9 will indicate students' expressed preferences among paired activities. A forced-choice devise could be developed that would yield students' preferences, ranging from strong preference to strong dislike.

Contrived Task Approach: Individual

The contrived task approach provides an assessment of skill functioning in conjunction with an estimate of reinforcement preference. It eliminates the necessity for obtaining separate information about a students' system of reinforcement and his academic achievement.

This approach to assessment of reinforcement begins by selecting a task believed to be easy for the child. As the child works on the assignment, the teacher applies a variety of potential reinforcers. Upon completion of the task, other reinforcers are tried. The student's performance is evaluated in terms of: 1) his enthusiasm for the task, 2) his persistence, and 3) the quality of his performance. The examiner then selects the reinforcer needed for this type of task. The cycle is repeated beginning with a more difficult assignment. Figure 4.10 shows the procedure.

FIGURE 4.10.   ASSESSMENT OF REINFORCEMENT: CONTRIVED TASK
                APPROACH

Procedure

1. Select a task (easy level)

Notes

1. Selected task: _____

_____

2. Try possible reinforcers   2. Reinforcements used: _____

    _____

    _____

3. Evaluate the performance   3. Performance
in terms of:

   a) child's enthusiasm   a) enthusiasm _____

   b) child's persistence   b) persistence _____

   c) quality of performance   c) quality _____

4. Select type of reinforcer   4. Type of reinforcer to use:
for this kind of task

    _____

    _____

5. Repeat cycle, using a   5. See 1 - 4
more difficult task.

This procedure yields information concerning:

1. Tasks that are easy for a child
2. What is reinforcing for him when doing easy tasks.
3. Tasks that he finds difficult.
4. What is reinforcing for him when he is confronted with difficult tasks.

This narrative, between Joan (see Chapter One) and a teacher, depicts the use of the contrived task approach when assessing Joan's reward system.

Teacher: (after having developed rapport) Joan, read this story to yourself. When you are finished, I'm going to ask you questions about it. If there are any words you don't know, ask me and I'll help you.

               (Joan begins reading a story written at a beginning third grade level that is printed on a card. As she reads, the examiner applies close physical proximity and a smile.)

Teacher: (after Joan has finished reading the selection) What did the boys build in the woods?

Joan: They built a house.

Teacher: Correct. What was under the table?

Joan: Some apples.

Teacher: You're right again! You have a good memory. What happened to the apples?

Joan: (Smiling) Two pigs ate them.

Teacher: (Winking) My, you read that story well, Joan.

Joan: (Joan smiles)

> Teacher records:
> a)   enthusiasm — little, seems disinterested
> b)   persistence — unwillingly completed selection
> c)   quality — answered 3 out of 3 questions.
>
> Teacher records:
> a)   withdraws from physical contact (touch)
> b)   likes verbal praise
> c)   responds favorably to winking

Teacher: (selecting a story at an early level) Now read this story to yourself.

Contrived Task Approach: In Groups

Just as tasks can be contrived and assigned to individual students for purposes of assessment, a similar approach can be used with small groups. The type of tasks may have to differ from those used with individual students because prerequisites for the tasks must be within the repertory of each group member. Also, fewer school related tasks lend themselves to group endeavors.

There are a number of advantages in using the Contrived Task Approach with a group. It can serve as a natural outgrowth of group activities and it provides valuable observations of group interactions. Group responses can serve as models for individuals who otherwise would be prone not to participate. The types of tasks that can be contrived for use with groups are:

Games and physical education activities
Problem solving tasks
Class discussion
Sensitivity training and group dynamics
Arts and crafts activities

Procedures for assessment of behavior and reinforcement through the Contrived Task Approach in groups is similar to that same approach as used with individuals. Figure 4.11 depicts the steps that are used in this process.

FIGURE 4.11. GROUP ASSESSMENT OF ACHIEVEMENT AND REINFORCE-
MENT: CONTRIVED TASK APPROACH

Procedures	Notes
1. Select a task that can be managed for all group members.	1. Indicate the task: _____ _____

2. Try possible reinforcers:
   a) social
   b) contingency
	2. Indicate reinforcers used:
	   a)
	   b)

3. Evaluate the performance in terms of:
   a) group's expressed interest
   b) persistence
   c) quality of performance — note any individuals who excelled or performed deficiently
	3. Evaluation of:
	   a)
	   b)
	   c)

4. Repeat cycle using a more difficult task, if necessary.	4. See 1 - 3

The description that follows is an example using the Contrived
Task Approach with a group of eight children ages 8 to 11.

Teacher: Boys and girls now we are going to work together on this
large mural. Each of you will be asked to help paint it. (At
this point the teacher assigns a designated area to be completed by each student.)

Teacher: Now that you have finished painting, you should all be proud
of the fine mural that you helped make. Where shall we place
it so that others can see it?

Teacher: How many of you would like to do something like this again?
(At this point, the teacher leads a group discussion concerning the student's feelings toward such a task.)

Note the steps followed by the teacher in the above example.
First an assignment was selected that was believed to be within the

attainment of each pupil. While they were painting, the teacher observed and noted the enthusiasm, persistence, and quality of work displayed by each child.

Secondly, the teacher applied social reinforcers (praise) as well as what could later be used as a contingent type of reward ("Where shall we place it so that others can see it?").

Third, the groups' attitude toward the task was evaluated by letting them discuss their product. The teacher could also evaluate the effects of the reinforcers by observing reactions when praise was used and when offering to display the mural.

As a result of using this assessment technique, the teacher has a better knowledge of the group. The children's interest in this type of task; the kind of reinforcement that appeals to them when faced with such an undertaking; and their level of accomplishment have been determined. The teacher also had an opportunity to acquire similar information about individual children.

Assessment of Reinforcement Rate

Frequency of reinforcement is an important characteristic to assess because the pay-off for responses dictates the repetitiveness with which they will reoccur. When an individual can maintain responses without external rewards, the act itself is reinforcing. Such a condition is the goal of Directive Teaching. But for those responses that have not yet become internalized, reinforcers external to the task are essential for the continued emission of responses.

Rate of reinforcement can be assessed through observation. Assessing reinforcement rate through the Contrived Task Approach is discussed here. Figure 4.12 contains a form used for assessing rate of reinforcement.

FIGURE 4.12. ASSESSMENT OF REINFORCEMENT RATE: CONTRIVED
　　　　　　　　TASK APPROACH

Student _____

Date _____

Procedures　　　　　　　　　*Notes*

1. Contrive a task —easy　　1. Task _____
   level

2. Try a secondary level reward. Set a given rate.	2. Secondary response _____
3. Observe response	3. Observation rate _____
4. Change the rate	4. Change rate _____
5. Observe response	5. Response _____
6. Repeat #4 if necessary	6. See 1 - 5
7. Evaluate the child's performance:	7.
a. motivation	a. _____
b. persistence	b. _____
c. quality of performance	c. _____
8. Select rate of response	8. Selection of rate _____

The reader should note that the steps shown in Figure 4.12 follow the previously described approach used when contriving a task for determining types of reward. After learning the procedure, it is relatively easy to assess rate of reinforcement simultaneously with an assessment of the type of reward. Initially, it is recommended that each assessment be conducted separately. After perfecting both, the two assessments can be combined into one process.

Summary

Directive teaching relies upon accurate, descriptive, and behaviorally relevant information about children with learning and behavioral handicaps. Such information is sometimes available from school records but more often must be obtained by teachers or other school personnel. Among other requirements, the information must be current if it is to be instructionally valuable.

Specific information about academic achievement should be gathered first. This assessment should focus on students' areas of academic difficulties. After acquiring data about academic performance, these findings are used as content for assessing expressive modalities and reward systems.

In-school behavior, relevant to teaching includes responses to instruction, to others, and to assignments. These responses are observable and can be obtained without the use of inferences.

The reward system is comprised of types of rewards and rate of reinforcement. Techniques for assessing reward systems include interviewing, using contrived tasks in conjunction with observations, and using paper-pencil forms.

Using Descriptive Information

Directive teaching is a system of instruction **FIVE** that aids those who teach children display-ing learning and behavioral difficulties to be effective in academic instruction while simultaneously responding to the students' social behavior. Because all complex behavior is learned, distinctions be-tween academic learning and other forms of in-school behavior are made only for purposes of describing instructional applications. Consequently, the term *behavioral task*[1] is used here to mean a required act that, when mastered, results in a change in behavior Included under behavioral tasks are: 1) academic learning tasks and 2) social learning tasks. These are discussed in the present chapter.

Directive teaching consists of three steps. First, it is necessary to gather descriptions of instructionally relevant behavior concerning academic functioning, social learning, and reinforcement systems of students. Second, this information is used for planning and imple-menting strategies that affect teaching and management of students. These strategies are instructional treatments used by teachers in an effort to improve student functioning. Third, the instructional treat-

---

[1] For an extensive discussion of a learning task, see Frank M. Hewett, *The Emotionally Disturbed Child in the Classroom* (Boston: Allyn & Bacon, Inc., 1968).

ment is evaluated simultaneously with its application. Its effects are reflected in changes in descriptive information.

Thus, a cycle of change results from directive teaching as shown in Figure 5.1. Once started, the system becomes self-generating. It provides for measurements that are embedded in the instruction.

FIGURE 5.1. THREE STEPS IN DIRECTIVE TEACHING

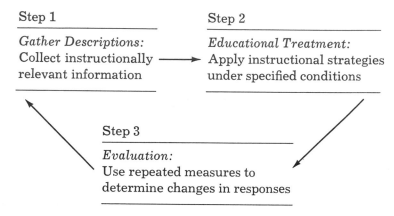

Step 1

Gather Descriptions:
Collect instructionally ⟶ relevant information

Step 2

Educational Treatment:
Apply instructional strategies under specified conditions

Step 3

Evaluation:
Use repeated measures to determine changes in responses

These, in turn, point up changes in functioning (Step 1) and result in a change in instructional strategy (Step 2) which again is measured (Step 3). Step 1, gathering descriptions, is discussed in Chapter 4. Step 2 is presented in Chapter 6 and Step 3, evaluation, is described in Chapter 7. The present chapter is devoted to ways information is useful to teachers and serves as a prelude to the discussion in Chapter 6 concerning instructional treatment.

USING INFORMATION ABOUT INDIVIDUALS

Information about student, even when it is relevant, is valuable only if it is used. When information is collected routinely without predetermined purposes, it is less likely that it will be used than if the purposes are precisely defined in advance. We are concerned in this chapter with using the types of information about individual students that were discussed in previous chapters.

Once instructionally relevant descriptions have been accumulated, teachers have a basis for specifying tasks to be learned by students. Descriptive information about their reward systems help establish conditions under which learning can best occur.

Information About Academic Achievement

Analyses of academic performance reveal skills, principles, and concepts that are known and those that are yet to be learned. Teachers are better able to sequence instruction when the current information they have is used for setting academic tasks, developing teaching strategies, and establishing terminal criteria.

Setting Academic Learning Tasks

An academic task is defined here as a required act, the mastery of which results in acquiring subject matter, and is reflected by a change in responses (behavior). This is an academic task:

> Arithmetic Computation: Do multiplication problems with two place numbers in the multiplier.

The above example meets our definition of an academic task. Its mastery will enable the student to respond to multiplication problems correctly and by learning this skill he will have acquired academic subject matter.

Sub-tasks are steps in a series that lead to or comprise a task. The above academic task could be made up of several sub-tasks as follows: [2]

Sub-task One: Express numbers in expanded notation
$$(23 = 20 + 3).$$

Sub-task Two: Use expanded notations in multiplication with one place multipliers

$$\begin{array}{r} 23 \\ \times 3 \\ \hline \end{array} \qquad \begin{array}{r} 20+3 \\ \times\ 3 \\ \hline 9 \\ +60 \end{array}$$

Sub-task Three: Use expanded notations with two place multipliers

$$\begin{array}{r} 23 \\ \times 33 \end{array} \qquad \begin{array}{r} 20+3 \\ 30+3 \end{array}$$

Sub-task Four: Use expanded notations in thinking but write the problems in traditional form

$$\begin{array}{r} 23 \\ \times 33 \end{array}$$

---

[2] The author acknowledges the work of three students in developing these steps: Arlene Anthony, Eleanor Coombs, and Janet Fink.

Note that the foregoing sub-tasks lead to the academic task which served as an instructional goal. Carefully devised instructional materials present similar procedures. Youngsters with learning problems, however, often have gaps in academic skills, requiring their teachers to incorporate systematic steps into their instruction and to select segments of instructional materials from various sources. It is probable that gaps in academic skills would not have occurred, however, had systematic teaching of this sort been used initially.

An example of setting academic tasks based on descriptive information is presented below. These tasks in reading were set for Mark based on those instructional outcomes that were described in Chapter 2.

Task: Visual Discrimination of letters and words.

Sub-tasks: Visual discrimination of *w* and *m*.
Visual discrimination of *b* and *d*.
Visual discrimination of *p* and *q*.
Learn to read *was* and *saw*.
Learn recognition of 120 Dolch sight words
Learn to read consistently left to right.

Task: Learn the names of letters.

Sub-tasks: Name the letters *m, n, q, p, d,* and *b.*

Task: Auditory discrimination of letters.

Sub-tasks: Auditory discrimination of *th* from *d.*
Auditory discrimination of *bl* from *ba.*
Auditory discrimination of *f* from *v.*

Teaching Strategy

Teaching strategy is a plan that details which students will be taught, what they will be taught, and how they will be taught in order to achieve specified academic tasks. Developing a teaching strategy involves selecting instructional materials to be used and choosing particular teaching methods. Since most experienced teachers have developed their own teaching styles and tend to have favorite instructional materials, teaching strategies are often a matter of personal preference.

Other factors must also be considered when devising teaching strategies. For example, instructional material must contain that content needed to meet the academic tasks, while teaching ap-

FIGURE 5.2. TEACHING STRATEGY FORM

Student(s) __Mark__ Teacher __Miss Smith__ Date __May 4__ Time of Day __9:00 – 9:30__

Sub-Tasks	Materials	Presentation	Reinforcement Type	Reinforcement Rate	Evaluation Criteria	Results
1. w – m	cardboard letters and placemats	Match cardboard letters on place-mats.	praise: "very good"	every second correct response	sorts 10 w's and m's	
2. b – d	same as #1	same as #1	same as #1	same as #1	sorts 10 b's and d's	
3. p – q	same as #1	same as #1	same as #1	same as #1	sorts 10 p's and q's	
4. was – saw	Language Master sentences: I saw a dog. He was a good dog.	saw – was in red	peer recognition at completion of task		10 consecutive readings	

proaches should take advantage of the learner's strongest sensory modalities. Other considerations include the availability of instructional materials; access to teacher assistants; physical facilities for teaching; and the number of students to be taught. A teacher in a clinical setting where students are tutored may use strategies that would not be feasible when teaching groups of students.

Figure 5.2 shows a teaching strategy form designed to be used for planning and for teaching one lesson. It contains strategies used to teach four academic sub-tasks to Mark which are described more fully below.

Example:

Task: Visual discrimination of letters and words

  Sub-tasks:
1. Visual discrimination of w - m.
2. Visual discrimination of b - d.
3. Visual discrimination of p - q.

Teaching Strategy: Present ten large cut-outs of each letter and placemats with a letter drawn on each mat. Tell Mark to sort the letters placing the correct cut-out on the placemat displaying that letter. Upon completion of the sorting, Mark checks his results by reading each letter to the teacher aide.

  Sub-task:
4. Visual recognition of *was* and *saw*.

Teaching Strategy: Use the Language Master.[3] Print these sentences on cards:

I *saw* a dog.
He *was* a good dog.

Words to be learned will be shown in red. The others will be shown in black. As the cards pass through the machine, Mark will read the sentences after the Language Master announces them.

Another example, from information about Joan that was presented in Chapter 4, provides teaching strategies based on more detailed assessments.

The academic tasks set for Joan and further delineated by the sub-tasks are:

Task: Improve word recognition

  Sub-tasks: Immediate recognition of *make, where, your, well, went, want, made, you, there, will.*

---

[3] A machine that is programmed to emit language as the words are shown (Bell and Howell, Inc.).

Task: Improve word attack skills of three syllable words.

    Sub-tasks: Recognition of *vacation, holiday, somebody, general, electric.*

Task: Improve skill in addition of common fractions.

    Sub-tasks: Add $1/3 + 1/3$; $2/5 + 2/5$; $3/6 + 3/6$

Task: Subtract problems requiring regrouping.

    Sub-tasks: Subtract $25 - 16$; $72 - 69$; $151 - 127$; $77 - 49$

These sub-tasks are expected to be taught over a period of several days. For example, one session in arithmetic instruction could include the following:

Sub-task	*Material*	*Presentation*
learn to subtract: $10 - 9$ $12 - 10$ $20 - 13$ $25 - 16$ $72 - 69$	paper, pencil, 75 plastic chips	Present problems in written form one at a time; have student set up problem using chips; student will use chips to solve problem and record the answer.

Note that the first two sub-tasks ($10 - 9$; $12 - 10$) have been correctly calculated by Joan. These will be presented as a review and also to provide encouragement through success. Joan demonstrated a failure to understand the concept of tens in subtraction. This will be taught to her through explanations by the teacher as they work together.

Problems	*Explanations*
25 -16 ——— 9	Because 6 is greater than 5, we need more ones. A ten is taken from the twenty to give us 15. Now we can subtract 6 from 15 which is 9 and 10 from 10 is zero.
72 -69 ——— 3	In this problem we are taking six tens and nine ones (69) from seven tens and two ones (72). We need additional ones to take nine from two. So we take one ten from the seventy which gives us 12. Now we can take 9 from 12, leaving 3. Sixty from sixty is zero. The answer is 3.

During an explanation of tens in subtraction, plastic chips can be used to "prove the answer." As the teacher proceeds, the student is gradually given an opportunity to describe the process, ultimately explaining an entire problem without assistance. In this way, teacher behavior can provide a model for thinking by the student.

Academic instruction should be approached from the point of view of the learner rather than from the teacher's perspective. In addition to years of preparation, teachers have had many opportunities to apply their knowledge. Consequently, one should not ignore minute steps in the belief that they are unimportant. We should always recognize that students, particularly those who have difficulty learning, are often confused about basic processes and help with each step will serve to reduce confusion and fill gaps in their thinking.

Establishing Terminal Criteria

Teachers need a basis for determining if instructional gains are being made in order to know when to set new tasks and when to change teaching approaches. Terminal criteria are used to satisfy this need.

Criteria for evaluation of instruction should be established when a task is set. Mager (1962) has noted that:

> If we can specify at least the minimum acceptable performance for each objective, we will have a performance standard against which to test our instructional program; we will have a means for determining whether our programs are successful in achieving our instructional intent.[4]

Thus by establishing acceptable performance in advance of instruction, it is possible to determine effects of teaching and then have a basis for decisions relative to subsequent instructional steps. Terminal criteria should be stated in terms that are observable, rather than speculative. We should use terms that convey performance, i.e., "reads, does, solves, writes," etc.

Criteria should also contain specific numbers of units to be correctly completed or maximum amount of time to be used for successful completion of the tasks, if either or both are appropriate. The terminal criteria used with Mark follow on page 117.

The reader should note that the teaching strategy establishes conditions under which teaching and learning take place. These conditions are reflected in terminal criteria. For example, in order for

---

[4] Robert F. Mager, *Preparing Objectives for Programmed Instruction* (Palo Alto: Fearon Publishers, Inc., 1962), p. 44.

Tasks	Criteria
Visual discrimination of:	
1. w and m	1. correctly sorts 10 w and m cut-outs.
2. b and d	2. correctly sorts 10 b and d cut-outs.
3. p and q	3. correctly sorts 10 p and q cut-outs.
4. visual discrimination of was and saw	4. 10 consecutive correct readings of the two words as contained in the sentences.

Mark to meet the criteria in Task 4, he must read *was* and *saw* correctly under those conditions described above.

If Mark does not meet the criteria after one instructional period (let us say, he achieved 8 out of 10 on Task 4), the same instruction should be repeated in subsequent sessions under similar conditions, and applying the same criteria. When failure to meet criteria is excessive (that is, if Mark misses 9 out of 10 on Task 4), the teacher should select an easier task, since the amount of positive reinforcement for successful performance will be too small.

The evaluation section of Figure 5.2 provides criteria for measuring results of instruction. While terminal criteria are established in advance of instruction, the results are recorded following student achievement. In this way, student performance (results) can be compared with desired achievement (criteria).

Selecting Learning Modalities

Information concerning the sensory modalities students find most effective in learning particular responses is useful for instruction. Descriptions of assessing learning modalities in Chapter 4 indicated that expressions of learners can reveal if learning occurred when instruction relied on a designated sensory channel. Further, it is possible to determine which modalities are most effective for acquiring certain types of stimuli. The effectiveness of acquisition is measured by observing the quality of the learner's responses.

Questions to be considered when using information about a student's expressive modalities are:

Which modes are used most effectively by the student in expressing elements of those academic or behavioral tasks that will be taught?

Example:

Joan's discrimination of material presented haptically was good (see Chapter 4). This fact was used in teaching subtraction by including plastic chips among the instructional material. The chips serve to help Joan in attending to details and in counting devices.

Auditory discrimination was found to be good when assessing Joan's delayed recall of a story read to her. This performance was also taken into account when teaching subtraction by providing verbal explanations of each step.

Which modalities are needed in order to receive the desired instruction?

Example:

In the immediately preceding example, the auditory and haptic modes were used because Joan had demonstrated facility to learn through these channels and because they permit receiving arithmetic instruction. A prolonged reliance upon haptics for arithmetic instruction is inappropriate since it does not lend itself to learning more advanced arithmetic but it does allow some basic instruction.

A multi-sensory approach in teaching Mark is reflected in Figure 5.1 where materials are presented haptically, visually, and auditorily. This combination was deemed necessary because he demonstrated moderate deficiencies in learning through all modalities when used alone, yet no severe inadequacies were noted in the use of any one channel. By relying upon three channels, Mark will probably have a better opportunity to receive the instruction than if one sensory modality were used.

With some children however, a multi-sensory approach tends to interfere with learning. In such cases, interference can be reduced by not using those channels that seemingly add to the difficulty, particularly in the initial stages of learning. Later, after the task has been learned, it can be presented to the learner using several modalities.

Information About In-School Behavior

Information concerning student in-school behavior reveals types of responses that are emitted under particular conditions. These responses comprise observable behavior while conditions under which the behavior occurred are composed of stimuli, time of day, tasks required of the student, and physiological factors. After obtaining descriptions of behavioral responses that occurred under specific conditions, decisions can be made concerning directions and manner of desired changes.

Results of observed behavior and decisions for changing behavior are used to establish social learning tasks, select management strategies, and establish terminal criteria.

Setting Social Learning Tasks

A *social learning task* is a required act, the mastery of which results in a change of behavior in school. Student behavior involves learning academic matter which was discussed under the section concerned with using information about academic achievement of students. It also includes other behavior that relates to academic learning, such as attending to relevant stimuli. Social tasks in school include conforming to accepted patterns of behavior and are often referred to as student conduct.

It was established in Chapter 4 that Mark worked from 3 to 7 minutes on reading work book assignments. Beyond that time he annoyed other children by leaving his seat and moving around the classroom. Given this information, it is possible to specify the following tasks for Mark:

1. To persist at reading seat work until it is completed
2. To refrain from disrupting children during seat work assignments
3. To refrain from wandering around the classroom without permission

Selecting Management Strategy

Management approaches should be selected after consideration of the desirable behavior engaged in by the child and after knowledge of what is sufficiently reinforcing to encourage him to strive toward appropriate behavior. Three behavioral tasks for Mark can be achieved using these strategies:

Task 1: Complete reading seat work

Management Strategy:

> Assign work book material to Mark that is easy for him and of such quantity that it can be completed within 3 minutes. The teacher aide will go to him upon completion of the assignment and compliment Mark on his good performance (it was established that adults' praise was rewarding to Mark).
> Each day the amount of assigned material will be slightly increased so that ultimately the time interval for completion will exceed 7 minutes.

Task 2: Refrain from disrupting others while doing seat work.

Management Strategy:

The strategy for Task 1 will serve to accomplish this task, particularly after the time increment has been increased. In addition, the teacher aide will give Mark permission to draw and color a picture (another predetermined reward) while praising him. He will be told that because he is working quietly, without annoying others, he may draw.

Task 3: Refrain from walking about the classroom without permission.

Management Strategy:

Strategies for meeting Tasks 1 and 2 will also help to meet this task. After completion of the picture, Mark will again be praised for his desirable performance. He will be permitted to go to the library corner and select a book as a reward for staying in his seat and completing the coloring assignment.

It should be noted that social learning tasks could also be incorporated into those academic tasks as listed previously. While Mark engaged in academic tasks, these same behavioral outcomes could be met through praise for working quietly at his seat while he sorted letters and for not annoying other children.

Establishing Terminal Criteria

Outcome criteria for social learning tasks are established in the same way as are those for academic tasks. Criteria for the three tasks described for Mark are:

Tasks	Criteria
1. Complete reading seatwork assignments.	1. Completes assignments of at least 10 minutes duration.
2. Refrain from disrupting others during seatwork.	2. Completes seatwork of at least 10 minutes duration without disrupting others.
3. Refrain from leaving his seat without permission.	3. Leaves seat only with permission.

Because of the close relationships of Tasks 1 and 2, criteria for successful fulfillment of both are identical. By dividing Tasks 1 and 2, the teacher allows for positive reinforcement of Mark for completion of seatwork (Task 1) even if he does not meet the criteria for successful completion of Task 2. It is from such positive reinforcement that greater gains will be made.

Information About Reinforcement Systems

Information about students' reinforcement systems provides teachers with knowledge that is potentially useful. If used, it helps to encourage persistence in academic pursuits; to develop positive attitudes toward school; and to control and shape behavior. The application of such information involves specifying rewards to be issued under certain conditions and at given intervals.

Specifying Rewards

Rewards or reinforcers are related to a designated task. They should be just as specific as are the tasks to be performed. In the immediately preceding examples, each reinforcer is specified. In Task 1, for a successful performance, Mark is told that he worked well (compliment). Both praise and coloring are his rewards for the successful completion of Task 2. For his success in Task 3, Mark is praised and permitted to walk to a section of the room to select a book of his choice. The tasks along with the reinforcement are as follows:

Tasks	Type	Reinforcement	Rate
1. completes reading seatwork assignments	secondary	"You worked well."	at completion
2. refrains from disrupting others during seatwork	secondary	"You worked well without bothering others."	at completion
3. refrains from leaving his seat without permission	secondary	"You stayed in your seat, that's good."	at completion
	interim	"You may select a book from the library."	

By specifying rewards, teachers have more options remaining in case the effects of those particular rewards diminish. If praising Mark declines in power, other secondary and interim rewards can be used. Also pairing a neutral event or weaker reinforcer with a powerful reward is feasible when the reward is specific. Selection of a book by Mark may not, at first, be reinforcing but by associating that activity with praise and walking (both of which were viewed as rewards by Mark) the teacher has transferred the power of these rewards to a desirable event (book selection).

Figure 5.3 shows the type and rate of reinforcement used with Mark in teaching four academic subtasks. Verbal praise ("very good") was used in three of the sub-tasks. Initially, it was issued after every second correct response. Gradually the fixed rate was changed until reinforcement was provided once during each activity. The fourth sub-task is to be performed with reinforcement at completion. This schedule was chosen because observations had revealed that the use of the Language Master provided sufficient reinforcement to Mark for him to continue without additional support.

Timing of Rewards

The importance of timing when reinforcing responses cannot be over-stressed. Ideally, reinforcement should occur simultaneously with the desired behavior or as closely following the behavior as is feasible. In associative learning where the intent is to relate one event with another, close proximity is crucial. If one were teaching word recognition through association of known colors with unknown letter symbols, the teaching plan could be presented as follows:

Task	Terminal Criteria	Reinforcer
Recognition of: "look, Mark"	Reads: "Look, Mark, look," correctly without aid of colors	Teacher attention during instruction

The teaching strategy could follow this sequence:

Step 1:

> *Teacher:* (showing Mark two sheets of colored paper, one red and one blue) Mark, put your right hand on the red paper. (after Mark correctly complies) What color is this paper?
> *Mark:* Blue

Step 2:

> *Teacher:* You are going to learn to read two new words today. This word is *look*. Shall we write in red or blue on the paper?
> *Mark:* Write it in blue.
> *Teacher:* L-O-O-K spells Look. Copy *look* on the paper in blue.
> *Teacher:* This word says your name, *Mark* (Teacher spells the word and pronounces it.) I'll write *Mark* in red. Now you write *Mark* in red.

Step 3:

> *Teacher:* Now let's put these two words together. What do they say?
> *Mark:* Look, Mark.

Step 4:

> *Teacher:* That's right. Now here is another blue word (Look). How does the sentence read now?
> *Mark:* Look, Mark, Look.

Step 5:

> *Teacher:* Very good, Mark. Now see if you can read this same sentence written in pencil. (The teacher prints the sentence with a regular lead pencil, leaving the sentence in color on the desk to serve as a model.)
> *Mark:* Look, Mark, Look.

The next teaching task in this series would include teaching the sentence *Look, Mark, Look* within the context of a short story in an attempt to transfer the learning.

Timing is helpful. Note in the above example that the teacher immediately indicated that Mark had correctly read the sentence. When a response is wrong, quick notification of that fact by the teacher also serves to obviate the false association. In doing so, however, the teacher should take care not to be discouraging. It is necessary to be supportive when calling an error to a student's attention, particularly with those who have experienced many school-related failures. In the following excerpt, note the manner used by Lester's teacher when giving him immediate reinforcement to an incorrect response.

> *Teacher:* Lester, you almost spelled *capture* right. If we change the letter t and p, you will have it exactly correct (Lester had spelled capture: "catpure").

By responding to the incorrectly spelled word in this way, the teacher was able to: 1) notify Lester of the inaccurate spelling of the word and 2) encourage Lester to persist by indicating that he was not entirely wrong and, in fact, was nearly correct.

Rate of Reinforcement

The frequency of reward is, as was noted earlier, an important element when teaching. Reward serves as an encouragement and as a guide, it can let the learner know that he is on the right track and it also serves to inform the respondent when he is in error.

Heavy dosages of rewards are sometimes needed to entice the child to begin an activity as the teacher attempts to capture the student's interest. But as he becomes involved in the desired activity, frequency of emitting rewards is gradually decreased with an ultimate aim of no external rewards for that activity. As success on a given task becomes more frequent, reinforcement becomes a part of the activity and is then internalized, which is the most effective type of reward.

The rate to be used in issuing reinforcement should be indicated in the teaching plan. It may be specified in terms of time: "Every ten minutes;" or in terms of rate of response: "Every fifth correct response;" or upon completion of a task: "After the workbook assignment is finished."

Using a Directive Teaching Plan

Segments of a directive teaching plan can serve to summarize the use of descriptive information. Figure 5.3 refers to the tasks, criteria, reinforcement, and rates that were discussed in conjunction with the management and teaching of Mark. Note that the teaching plan shown in Figure 5.3 does not contain teaching and management strategies. It is viewed as useful over a longer period of time than are teaching and management strategies. These are often changed daily.

It may seem unnecessary to record in detail the tasks, terminal criteria, type and rate of reinforcement. However, teachers who use these procedures set a portion of each day aside for a systematic application of directed activities for which a careful plan should be designed. Subsequently, teachers often find themselves applying positive reinforcement in a more conscious fashion during other segments of the school day.

In a sense, the procedures that have been described in this and preceding chapters serve to help teachers to program themselves so that they become more systematic in response to the behavioral and learning problems that are evidenced by their students. The effectiveness of directive teaching can be measured by the extent to which this occurs during the course of the reader's teaching.

USING INFORMATION ABOUT GROUPS

Descriptive information can also be used to establish behavioral tasks for groups of students; to devise teaching and management strategies; and to specify terminal criteria. Procedural modifications

FIGURE 5.3. DIRECTIVE TEACHING PLAN

Student _____ Mark _____ Teacher _____ Mrs. Smith _____ Date _____ May 5 _____ Time _____ 9 - 9:30

Task(s)	Terminal Criteria	Reinforcer	Rate
Visual discrimination of:	Correctly sorts 10:	1, 2 and 3:	1, 2 and 3 at completion.
1. *w* and *m*	1. *w* and *m* cutouts	Upon completion of sorting:	4. During task performance, give "A" when criterion is met.
2. *b* and *d*	2. *b* and *d* cutouts	"Very good, you finished these all by yourself."	
3. *p* and *q*	3. *p* and *q* cutouts	Upon completion of reading:	
4. visual recognition of *was* and *saw*	4. ten consecutive correct readings of *was* and *saw* in sentences without aid of Language Master.	"You did very well, you knew X number of letters."	
		4. Teacher attention, use of Language Master, and an "A" in reading.	
1. do reading seatwork until completed	1. completes assignment	1. "You worked well."	1, 2 and 3 at completion of tasks
2. refrains from disrupting others during seatwork	2. completes assignment without annoying others	2. "You worked well without bothering others, you may color now."	
3. remains in seat while doing seatwork	3. does not leave seat without permission	3. "You stayed in your seat, that's good. You may select a book from our library."	

are necessary in order to apply directive teaching to groups. These adjustments include establishing tasks that are relevant to groups and using methods for reinforcing responses that are applicable in group settings.

Setting Tasks for Groups

It is essential that each group member has achieved a minimal level of functioning prior to being taught a particular task. If all members have not mastered the prerequisite skills for the tasks to be taught, they cannot be expected to learn the task and do not constitute a group that can profit from that particular instruction. Under these circumstances, the group is not properly organized for instruction. It should either be reconstituted or appropriate behavioral tasks should be selected for instruction.

Social learning tasks are often more readily applicable to group instruction than are academic learning tasks. While both types of tasks require prerequisite skills, the range of academic functioning within a group tends to be greater than that of social behavior. Due to this wider span of differences, teaching academic tasks to groups is often more difficult. Figure 4.8 contains information about a group of five boys in Miss Jackson's class. These boys will serve as an example of an instructional group.

Miss Jackson obtained the following information concerning the boys' reading word attack skills:

All members recognized these words by sight:

hill	bump	rain	sleep
wind	snow	room	

These words serve as prerequisite reading skills for tasks to be taught. In a test accompanying a basic reading series, Miss Jackson found that none of the boys recognized derivatives formed by adding the suffix y to the above root words. Thus, they did not recognize these words:

hilly	bumpy	rainy	sleepy
windy	snowy	roomy	

Miss Jackson established this academic task for the group.

Task: Recognize derivatives formed by adding the suffix y to: hill, bump, rain, sleep, wind, snow, room.

She also established terminal criteria to be used in evaluating student performance on the task.

Terminal criteria: Students will immediately recognize the italicized words in these sentences:

> This is *hilly* land.
> The road is *bumpy.*
> This is a *rainy* day.
> I am *sleepy.*
> It is a *windy* day.
> It was a dark, *snowy* night.
> We have a big *roomy* house.

Reinforcement with Groups

Issuing rewards to individuals within groups need not be different from providing reinforcement to one student. However, devices and techniques can be used to record and assist teachers in issuing rewards to students.

Timing devices can be used to permit students to have "time out" from work on an individual basis. With this system, students earn points (minutes) for certain specified tasks. These can be cashed in by the students upon request. The teacher or teacher assistant simply sets the timing device for the amount of time earned by the student. During this time interval, students may engage in a number of previously designated privileges such as table games, painting, or other play activities. When the time expires, the timer's alarm notifies the student to return to academic tasks.

Charts can be used to record numbers of points earned by students. Points are usually issued at the close of an activity. A master chart containing each student's name is displayed as a constant reminder to students. Sometimes records are also kept by each student so that they can note their progress.

Similarly, tokens have been used in lieu of points. These are issued to students for appropriate responses and are cashed in for rewards. When points, tokens, and other interim rewards are issued to students, these should be paired with praise and other forms of social reinforcement.

Figure 4.8 indicates that each member of Miss Jackson's group prefers different rewards. Based on this information, she established the following reinforcement schedule.

Reinforcement: Upon meeting terminal criteria, students will be given 15 minutes to engage in their stated preference.

Thus, Miss Jackson told the boys before beginning instruction that when they learned to read the seven new words they would be permitted to have fifteen minutes to do what they requested. Each reward was announced to the students prior to the lesson.

Summary

The use of descriptive information in directive teaching is used to set behavioral tasks; determine teaching and management strategies; and establish terminal criteria. Behavioral tasks are required acts that are reflected in a change in behavior when achieved. They consist of subtasks which are a series of steps leading to the mastery of a task.

Teaching and management strategies are activities that are designed to achieve tasks. Terminal criteria are used to evaluate changes in responses as a result of the teaching and management strategies.

Treatment Forms: Academic and Social Instruction

We must do more than merely label and explain a **SIX**
disorder if children with learning and behavioral
handicaps are to be helped. Attitudes and interests have changed
in this respect over the years, a fact to which Lewis Terman's words
attest:

> It had long been known that there were persons of otherwise
> normal intelligence who could not learn to read by any amount of
> ordinary school instruction. The condition was believed to be
> due to some congenital brain defect and to be hopelessly incur-
> able. Mental pathologists named the condition "word-blindness"
> or "alexia" (inability to read) and gave themselves little further
> concern about it. Dr. Fernald was the first to demonstrate beyond
> possibility of doubt that the most extreme cases of word-blindness
> are quickly and completely curable.[1]

Contemporary educational practitioners tend more toward treatment of learning problems than diagnosis. Although even today
vestiges of an earlier period in special education are frequently seen
when an undue emphasis is placed on diagnostic procedures to the
detriment of educational treatment.

---

[1] L. M. Terman, "Foreword," in *Remedial Techniques in Basic School Subjects,*
Grace Fernald (New York: McGraw-Hill Book Company, 1943), p. vii.

Similarly problems of behavioral adjustment were at one time either ignored or harshly treated depending upon the nature of the disruptive behavior. Compliant and quiet children often were ignored and thus encouraged to continue their maladaptive practices, but those manifesting acting-out and destructive behavior were severely dealt with in the schools. Over-reactions to the harshness of an earlier era are seen in pronouncements against all forms of discipline and control (Valentine, 1965). In addition to those who purposely apply measures for controlling student behavior and those who fail to use effective measures in managing students, there is another group of teachers who inadvertently reinforce undesirable behavior.

When teachers provide attention and other forms of reinforcement to students who display inappropriate behavior, they are unwittingly encouraging a repetition of that behavior. Teachers do not aim to develop inappropriate responses among their students, but without systematic procedures that include relevant instruction, it is difficult for them to modify behavior.

Teaching involves academic instruction as well as instruction in social behavior. As noted previously, teachers cannot separate academic instruction and management of students because effective teaching requires learners who attend and respond to relevant stimuli. Children whose poor academic skills reflect their defective academic learning and other in-school behavior need special treatment so that they can be responsive to school instruction and management. Help can be provided to students who have pronounced learning problems through approaches described under academic instruction and social instruction.

ACADEMIC INSTRUCTION

Academic instruction is aimed at improving students' functioning in the basic tool subjects and contributing to better in-school behavior. Rationales for using approaches derived from reinforcement theory should make clear to readers the value of these approaches.

Rationales for Using Reinforcement

The approaches described in this text help children with learning problems in at least five ways. Each is listed below followed by an example.

1. Specificity of task. By specifying each task to be learned, teachers are assisted in becoming more systematic when teaching. Specificity provides students with a sequence of instruction that begins with elements of tasks that they perform correctly. In this way teachers build on success which is a powerful reward.

Example:

Mrs. Hammon analyzed results of the California Achievement Tests that were administered to her class by using the diagnostic analysis form that accompanies the test (see Figure 4.1) she noted that four of her male students failed 15 or more of 20 test items that measured subtraction. She decided to teach these four boys subtraction as a special group.

First she devised a short test of simple subtraction problems. From the results, she determined which subtraction skills each boy did and did not do correctly. These are summarized in Figure 6.1. Note that none of the four students correctly subtracted problems that required bridging (i.e., $11-6$).

FIGURE 6.1. SUMMARY OF SUBTRACTION SKILLS OF FOUR STUDENTS

Student	Subtracts Zero from Whole No.	Subtracts Correctly
Fred	to ten	all numbers from 10
Harry	to ten	all numbers from 8
Tom	to ten	all numbers from 10
Mike	to ten	all numbers from 9

Next Mrs. Hammon set up an arithmetic task and evaluative criteria as follows:

Task	Criteria
Subtract all numbers below 10.	Add and subtract all numbers correctly within the concept of 10.

This task contains some elements that are within the behavioral repertoire of each boy. For Fred and Tom it will serve as a review since they previously demonstrated subtraction of all numbers below ten. Because Mrs. Hammon plans to extend instruction beyond the concept of ten, she believes a review will aid all group members and will serve to establish a cooperative spirit among the boys.

2. Association of Responses. Through reinforcement of correct responses students learn to associate these answers with a particular task or stimulus. In this way children learn that a printed symbol represents a particular sound and that a word or groups of words denote concepts.

When teachers use positive rewards, students associate good feelings with academic instruction and may extend these feelings to schooling in general. Children tend to persist more willingly in academic endeavors because of these positive feelings. Providing students with immediate feedback as to the correctness or error of their responses is also reinforcing.

Example:

Based on observations of the four boys, Mrs. Hammon uses success as a reward in addition to immediate feedback about the accuracy of their responses as well as group recognition through verbal praise.

The reward scheme is:

Reward	*Rate*
Success	When it occurs
Feedback	After every response
Praise	At the completion of the lesson

Feedback after each response is used to establish associations with correct answers to a given problem. *Success* and *praise* are used to develop positive attitudes in the boys toward arithmetic. The following narrative describes Mrs. Hammon's teaching strategy.

Mrs. Hammon: (with a large box of buttons in the center of the table) Look at the first problem on the board, (8−1.) Read the problem aloud, Mike.

Mike: Eight take away one.

Mrs. Hammon: That's correct, Mike.

Mrs. Hammon: Each of you take ten buttons from the box. (She checks to make certain each boy took the correct number of buttons.) Use your buttons to solve the problem shown on the board. How many buttons do you need to do the problem, Fred?

Fred: Eight

Mrs. Hammon: That's correct Fred. Explain how you know we need eight buttons.

Fred: The larger number is eight and we'll take one from it.

Mrs. Hammon· Each of you count eight buttons and place them in front of you.

Mrs. Hammon: (after checking to ascertain that each boy correctly counted eight) Now take one button away from eight.

Mrs. Hammon: Tom, how many buttons do you have remaining?

Tom: Seven

Mrs. Hammon: Yes, Tom. One from eight leaves seven. Now, each of you write the problem on your papers.

Mrs. Hammon: (after having completed the eights and nines) You boys did very well in arithmetic today. All of the problems we had were done correctly.

3. Shaping responses. Clues to appropriate responses encourage learners to continue toward successful completion of tasks and provide them with positive reinforcement. Notice in the example below how Mrs. Hammon presents problems in such a way that correct answers are almost guaranteed.

Example:

Mrs. Hammon: Yesterday we learned how to think through and work subtraction problems. We used buttons yesterday. Today I want you to draw circles to explain your problem. For example, the first problem is "ten take away one." Your drawing should look like this (at this point she draws two sets of five circles each on the chalkboard). We take one away by drawing an X over one circle (demonstrated on the chalkboard).

Mrs. Hammon: Now without calling out the answer count the number of remaining circles and write the answer on your paper.

Mrs. Hammon: Harry, how many circles remain?

Harry: Nine

Mrs. Hammon: That's right Harry. Very good. So, ten take away one leaves how many, Mike?

Mike: Nine

Mrs. Hammon: Good. I see each of you got the right answer.

Mrs. Hammon: Mike, here is another problem. You draw the circles on the board and do the problem while the rest of you boys do it at your seats. Ten take away three. Do the problem, Mike, and show us how you got your answer.

Mike: Seven. Three (pointing to his drawing) from ten leaves seven.

Mrs. Hammon: Seven is right. Very good.

4. Strengthening responses. By gradually decreasing rate of reinforcement, students' persistence and positive attitudes toward the activity are strengthened. After students demonstrate their interest

and feelings of mastery over the task of subtracting from ten, rate of reward for the special arithmetic group was changed to this:

Reward	Rate
Feedback	At the completion of ten problems
Praise	At the close of the lesson

Example:

> Mrs. Hammon: (after introduction of the assignment) Do the ten problems on your paper; when you are finished put the paper here and begin working on your spelling assignments.

> Mrs. Hammon: (after each member of the group has completed assignment) I looked over your papers and you each did a very good job. Now let's talk about each problem together.

In the above example, the teacher had moved the children from a fixed rate of reinforcement, providing praise and feedback for every ten correct responses through evaluation at completion of the assignment.

5. Observable outcomes. Students and teachers see the immediate effects of instruction because terminal criteria for success are set in advance and are specific.

Criteria were established by Miss Hammon for the special group in arithmetic. She initially indicated to them what would be taught or reviewed and routinely pointed out what each of them had accomplished. When the criteria had been met by the entire group, she reminded the boys that they had been working toward mastery of subtraction of numbers to ten and subtraction from ten.

These five reasons for using reinforcement principles when responding to student behavior are reflected in instructional goals that have long been sought by many teachers. Attainment of such goals, however, has often eluded teachers of children with learning and behavioral handicaps. A quick and easy way to meet instructional goals for these children still does not exist but the trend toward using approaches derived from reinforcement theory provides a promising direction.

Teaching Prerequisites

Teachers who use remedial approaches in assisting children with learning problems have relied for years on techniques based on reinforcement principles (Brueckner, 1935). A remedial approach typically involves determining those elements in skill areas the student has not yet mastered. These prerequisites are then taught in some sequential fashion. Remedial instruction has been defined as: *teaching that is reserved for a small number of children who are severely handicaped in the achievement of basic skills and who are in need of individual attention* (Otto and McMenemy, 1966, p. 35).

Included by some remedial specialists, and currently in vogue, is a rationale for an eradication of or a diminution of the "underlying causes" of learning failures. Teachers have been encouraged by some writers to engage students in a myriad of exercises in order to improve such things as: visual perception; motor skills; eye-hand coordination; emotional adjustment; language skills; ability to generalize; and a host of other known or suspected causes of learning handicaps. Such treatment has its roots in diagnostic procedures that focus on presumed causes of learning problems and labeling of disorders with a tendency to assume that diagnosis is fundamental to instruction. Many who prescribe treatment of this kind are not teachers. Usually they are specialists from areas allied to teaching such as psychology, medicine, and optometry. Such treatment is reminiscent of medical practice where a cause-effect relationship is often found through diagnostic procedures. Academic instruction however, should be based upon those prerequisite skills needed for acquiring a given body of information, academic skills, or tasks.

Skills that are directly related to tasks have been improved through instruction but general skill training, such as psychomotor training, is of questionable value probably because such training is often isolated from meaningful academic tasks. There is good reason to question the existence of a general psychomotor ability. Studies using the technique of factor analysis have failed to isolate such abilities (Fleishman and Hempel, 1956).

Assessment procedures based on observations of responses to academic tasks produce information that is more valuable for teaching than do diagnostic procedures that rely upon inferences and, in many instances, upon hypothetical constructs.

Remedial instruction is the most direct route to improving defective academic skills when the teacher recognizes those prerequisite skills needed to learn what is to be taught. Under these circumstances, instruction begins after determining that segment of academic skills the student has not mastered; that which he has acquired; and that in which he has demonstrated the prerequisites to learn. It is also necessary to know which learning modalities provide ready access for mastery of what is to be taught. After this information has been obtained, teaching should begin at a point below that which has been mastered. By starting instruction at a lower skill level, students have an opportunity to review prerequisites for the next level of difficulty and also to receive positive reinforcement for their successes.

These procedures require that teachers have a thorough knowledge of the sequence of academic skills; they must know which skills are prerequisites to other academic skills. Furthermore, they must recognize flaws in learning that may be disguised by superficial responses, or verbiage that interfere with the smooth acquisition of more difficult skills and concepts.

Teachers of children with learning and behavioral problems must be skillful in assessing academic functioning or have ready access to others who are competent to do assessment. The notion of using contrived tasks, as described earlier in this text, serves as an example of one type of assessment. Teachers who are assessment oriented continually evaluate performances and responses of students and, as a result, modify their techniques and demands.

When shifts in the levels of instruction and teaching approaches are indicated by mastery of tasks, teaching should take place in an orderly and systematic fashion. Consistency, with gradual increments in difficulty of academic content, is an essential ingredient of remedial instruction.

Directive teaching implies that students will be taught what is clearly relevant to their learning problems. As indicated previously, training without regard to subject matter will not result in improved academic skills. Rather, if the goal of instruction is to improve academic functioning, the teacher should use content that is a part of the desired skill.

Consequently, a frontal attack on learning problems is advocated. This direct approach contains two features:

1) teaching specific elements and
2) using when possible the child's strongest sensory-expressive mode for teaching those elements.

Teach Specific Elements

Academic skills are to a great extent cumulative; in order to learn one segment, that which precedes it must already be known. Word attack skills and arithmetic computation skills exemplify the notion of a hierarchy of skills. For example, the concept of ten must be understood in order to bridge or borrow when subtracting numbers. Let us return to Mrs. Hammon and the special remedial arithmetic group in order to illustrate both the need to understand the sequence of skills and the importance of teaching specific elements.

The instructional task of subtracting all numbers below 10 was selected by Mrs. Hammon. This computational skill was taught to the four boys even though two of them demonstrated a knowledge of subtracting all numbers below ten and the other two boys (Harry and Mike) achieved the skill to 8 and to 9 respectively. But Mrs. Hammon retaught these subtraction facts in order to: a) make certain the boys had mastered them, b) to reinforce positive responses, and c) to get them to begin working as a group. It is imperative, of course, that the students have the concepts of 8 and 9 well in mind in order for them to learn the concept of ten.

After the review, which has already been described, of subtracting all numbers from 8 and 9, Mrs. Hammon began to teach Harry and Mike the concept of ten and to review this concept with Fred and Tom. The teaching tasks and evaluative criteria are as follows:

Tasks	*Criteria*
1. learn the concept of 10	1. a) counts to 10 b) places ten objects in a group to represent 10
2. learn to add all combinations of 10	2. adds all combinations of 10
3. learn to subtract all numbers from 10	3. subtracts all numbers from 10

These tasks and criteria reflect the teacher's understanding of sequence in arithmetic computational skills. She realizes that to understand and use the concept of ten the learner must know the number names to ten in order (counts to ten) and he must know that ten ones constitute ten. Mrs. Hammon also recognizes that addition typically precedes subtraction. She is therefore reteaching the addition facts to ten, although the four students had demonstrated mastery of addition to ten. Through the inclusion of addition, the teacher provides for practice and review as well as opportunities to perform easy tasks that lend themselves to success.

The teaching strategy to be used by Mrs. Hammon for the first task "the concept of ten," serves to show one way of teaching specific elements.

Teaching Strategy

Instructional Materials:

Ten pennies and one dime for each boy, forty pennies and four dimes in all; paper and pencil brought to the group by each boy; chalkboard and chalk.

Presentation:

Each student will be given a dime (check to make sure each knows that it represents 10 cents); the container of 40 pennies will be placed in the center of the table, each boy will be asked to change his dime for 10 pennies; they will be asked: how many pennies in 10 cents? How can you check your answer?

Activities:

Draw 10 circles on your paper as I do it on the board: write the number 10 next to your circles; write the number one below each circle; how many ones do you have? Count them.

Evaluation:

At the close of the lesson combine all 40 pennies; have each child remove the pennies counting one at a time aloud and pile the pennies in groups of ten.

Use of Sensory Modes

Teachers of children with learning problems should capitalize on those modalities that provide the most direct routes to learning specified tasks. Those sensory channels that are demonstrably effective as receptors for the student in an academic skill should be used whenever possible. The position advocated herein is that success contributes to further success. Consequently, a weak sensory mode should only be used when it is essential because of the nature of the task and then only in conjunction with the child's strongest channel of learning.

Certain sensory modes are better used than are others for assimilating particular instruction. It should be recognized that the senses of smell and touch may have limited uses for schooling.

Olfaction does not lend itself to teaching abstractions because odors emanate only from matter. The haptic sense is also a limited channel for academic instruction because one cannot feel abstractions and because school materials are heavily oriented toward vision and hearing. Even with these limitations, the olfactory and haptic modes have not been utilized in the classroom as much as is possible. With the rapid change in technology, equipment and materials may hopefully be developed for taking advantage of olfaction and haptics in teaching.

We return to the group of four boys that are receiving special instruction in arithmetic. Assessment of their learning modes was accomplished using content in arithmetic. The results are shown in Figure 6.2. Olfaction was not assessed in this instance because of its limited utility in arithmetic instruction.

FIGURE 6.2. RESULTS OF ASSESSMENT OF LEARNING MODES OF FOUR BOYS WITH DEFICITS IN ARITHMETIC SKILLS

Mode	Discrimination			Recall Immediate			Recall Delayed		
	+	−	0	+	−	0	+	−	0
Auditory:	Fred Tom	Mike	Harry	Fred Tom		Mike Harry	Fred Tom	Harry	Mike
Visual:	Tom Fred Harry		Mike	Tom Fred Harry		Mike	Fred	Harry	Tom Mike
Haptics:	Mike Tom Harry			Harry	Tom Fred	Mike	Fred Mike		Tom Harry

The descriptions of teaching that follow deal with using a prominent or strong sensory mode, and a weak but essential sensory mode.

Sensory channels that are most effective in acquiring academic skills should be used whenever possible. The teacher, when deciding which modality to rely upon for instruction, should take into consideration the nature of the material and the results of the student's performance in the assessment of expressive learning. For example when visual discrimination of words and recall of reading matter are adequate, the vision channel should be emphasized for reading instruction.

Example:

Assessment of sensory learning indicated that Tom, Fred, and Harry discriminate arithmetic symbols accurately through the visual mode. Arithmetic instruction for these boys should rely upon visual materials. Because Tom's delayed recall of visual material is below criterion level and his delayed recall of auditory learning is above criterion level his arithmetic instruction should pair auditory input with visual stimuli.

A sensory mode that is demonstrably inadequate for acquisition of stimuli in a given subject area may need to be used when an academic skill can be acquired only through a particular sensory channel, such as the reliance of vision for reading print. A sensory mode that is more proficient in assimilating particular stimuli should be used to supplement or in association with a less efficient but necessary channel.

Example:

Assessment of sensory learning showed that Mike's auditory discriminations were below criterion and that his visual discriminations were at criterion, while haptic discriminations were above the criterion score. Therefore, skills in arithmetic computation will be taught to Mike using the chief sensory channels (vision and auditory) supplemented by haptics.

Teaching strategies are indicated that involve manipulating objects in conjunction with arithmetical symbols that are visual. The aforementioned teaching strategy using coins and symbols serves as an example of tying haptics to visual and auditory stimuli.

A multi-channel approach is particularly important with Mike because he demonstrated average immediate recall and above criterion delayed recall of arithmetical stimuli that were presented haptically. But his delayed recall of visually presented material was below criterion. By repeated instruction of the same skill or concept over shortly spaced periods of time, delayed recall of arithmetic should be improved.

SOCIAL INSTRUCTION

Behavioral responses that occur within a teacher-learner context comprise types of behavior discussed in this text. In Chapter 4, three groups of in-class behaviors were presented. These are: reactions to instruction; reactions to others; and reactions to assignments.

Basic behavioral requirements essential for learning in school include: 1) attending behavior; 2) following directions; 3) participating behavior; and 4) practice and self-instruction.

1. *Attending Behavior.* Children must attend to stimuli in order to acquire academic skills. These often are of an auditory or visual form. Student behaviors involve *listening* to teachers, to recordings, and to fellow students. Behaviors involving vision may require attending to printed matter, television, or film.

2. *Following Directions.* Learners follow directions that are presented auditorily or visually. Behaviors may involve completing an assignment as directed and following specified rules of conduct. Students who willingly follow directions are engaging in behavior that is acceptable and, hopefully, relevant. Those who refuse to follow directions and will not, for example, open their programmed texts cannot profit from this form of instruction.

3. *Participating Behavior.* Interactions with others are part of group instruction. Appropriate behavior in groups requires individuals to accommodate their impulses to demands of other group members. Not only must students follow rules and directions that pertain to the group but they must also share time, materials, and attention with others.

4. *Practice and Self-Instruction.* Students, particularly those with learning and behavioral handicaps, make gains in academic skills through practice and self-initiated instruction. Those who use the academic skills that they are in the process of acquiring are engaging in behavior that will serve to generalize their learnings beyond the classroom.

Persistence is another important behavior that contributes to learning. Children who willingly practice school related activities tend to learn more rapidly than those with similar learning problems who display less persistent behavior.

Approaches to Teaching Appropriate Social Behavior

Actions of teachers determine greatly how children behave in school and how they respond to instruction. Peers are also powerful influencers of student behavior. As teachers respond to students their behavior will be strengthened and tend to reappear, and when responses are not reinforced they become less frequent. Both appropriate and inappropriate responses are elicited or extinguished by teachers often without their awareness. The discussion in this section deals with approaches that teachers can use to encourage desirable behavior and to change undesirable responses.

Suggestions for Developing Desirable Behavior

Systematic use of positive reinforcement will reduce the need for using aversive techniques because rewards serve to encourage behavior. As more desirable behavior is emitted inappropriate responses become less frequent. Thus, inappropriate behavior is changed and less time is available for it to occur. Desirable behavior can be developed and maintained by applying the following suggestions.

Use Positive Reinforcement / Teachers often want to show children how to respond in appropriate ways. They want to be in a position to provide positive reinforcement, that is, reward for acceptable behavior, as opposed to punishment for unacceptable behavior. In order to issue positive reinforcement, several conditions should be present.

First, teachers must have knowledge of what students view as reinforcing. They should know what is rewarding to each child and under which conditions the rewards will be effective.

Second, responses to be rewarded must be elicited by teachers or responses must be so clearly defined that they will be evident to teachers upon appearance.

Third, reinforcement must occur when desired behavior or reasonable approximations of it are demonstrated.

Fourth, desired behavior should be systematically reinforced. It is important that teachers be consistent in replying to behavior; desired responses should not be punished or ignored inadvertently. By responding to behavior in either of these ways, teachers may extinguish the very responses they are seeking to develop.

Fifth, schedules of reinforcement should be established so that behaviors are not extinguished through insufficient reinforcement or satiated from excessive reinforcement. A recommended practice to follow is to reward newly emitted desired responses frequently at first. After behaviors have become established, vary the frequency of the rewards.

Example:

Readers will recall Lester (Chapter 1) and his emission at frequent intervals of animal-like sounds. The following *behavioral* tasks were planned by his teacher, Mrs. Crown, to be taught to Lester in conjunction with reading instruction:

1. To respond appropriately in reading group.

2. To refrain from making animal-like sounds while working independently in reading.

Mrs. Crown established terminal criteria for these two tasks as follows:

1. Lester will participate in reading group, evidencing appropriate responses for 10 consecutive days.
2. Lester will not make inappropriate sounds during silent reading and work book activity time for 10 consecutive days.

Observations of Lester's reward system indicated he liked Mrs. Crown to place her hand on his head whereupon he responded with a smile. With such attention, Lester behaved as desired for as long as 20 minutes and as little as 8 minutes. Further observations suggested that smiles from the teacher were mildly reinforcing and verbal praise seemed to be of neutral influence. The segment of the plan concerned with reinforcers and rate follows:

Reinforcer	*Rate*
1. Pat, paired with a smile and verbal praise.	1. When responding properly to a question.
2. Same as 1 (above) alternate pat, smile, and praise.	2. Every 7 minutes, gradually withhold until end of period.

Strategy for the implementation of the directive teaching plan for Lester is shown below.

In reading group. Begin discussion of story with a question that Lester can answer. Direct the question to him. After he correctly answers the question, pat him, smile, and praise him.

Midway through the discussion, if Lester has not volunteered a response, direct another question to him, following the same procedure as above. The last question in the discussion will also be devised for Lester. In this way, he will start off the session with positive reinforcement, get support during the lesson and receive a "booster shot" at the close of the period.

Example:

Mrs. Crown: (speaking to three children in a reading group) You boys are to be congratulated for reading today's story so quietly (said loudly so other children in the room can hear). We're now going to talk about what you read. Remember our rules in group discussion. Harry what is rule one?

Harry: (whose hand was raised) Put our hands up. Don't shout!

Mrs. Crown: Lester what is the title of our story today?

Lester: (after looking at the chalkboard to ascertain from the title printed on the board if he did recall correctly) "Department Stores."[2]

Mrs. Crown: Yes, that's correct. That is another right answer for you Lester. (Teacher smiles and pats Lester who is seated next to her.) All of you are paying attention very well. Let's see who can answer the next question.

Mrs. Crown: After you find the part in the story that describes what is in the windows of Deal's Department Store raise your hand.

Mrs. Crown: (after waiting for the three boys to raise their hands) Mike you read aloud. Lester and Harry will read silently. (As Mike reads Lester makes a squealing sound. Harry laughs but Mike continues reading.)

Mrs. Crown: Mike you found the section concerning the articles in the window of Deal's Department Store and you read perfectly. You certainly follow directions well!

Mrs. Crown: What were some of the items in the windows? (noting that Lester has raised his hand) Lester?

Lester: Pillows, shirts and clothes.

Mrs. Crown: Find the part that describes things to eat that are sold in *some department stores*[3] Harry. While he is reading, Lester and Mike try to count to yourselves the number of foods that are mentioned.

Mrs. Crown: (after Harry has finished reading) Harry read very well. Each of you boys are behaving and working fine today.

Mrs. Crown: Lester write the foods that you counted on the board over here. And Mike put the words that you found about food here. You may use your books to find the correct spelling of the words. Harry, you find the three words in the story that are names of things used in department stores for going from one floor to another and write them on the board here.

Mrs. Crown: (after checking each student's work) Lester listed four words that represent food. And each is correctly spelled (smiling and patting Lester's shoulder). Mike you listed four words also.

---

[2] Charles C. Fries, Rosemary G. Wilson, and Mildred K. Rudolph, "Department Stores," in *Merrill Linguistic Readers: Reader 6* (Columbus, Ohio: Charles E. Merrill Publishing Co., 1966), pp. 104–105.

[3] The phrase *some department stores* serves as a clue since the paragraph to be read begins with these words.

Very good. And three of them are spelled correctly (as she helps Mike spell *bread* correctly).

Mrs. Crown: Let's talk about the three words that Harry listed (stairs, elevator, and escalator).

Mrs. Crown: (following the discussion) I want to congratulate each of you for behaving so well during our reading group. Your reading has improved because you are paying attention.

During Seatwork. Begin with all three reinforcers every 7 minutes. On the second day, withhold reinforcement for 8 minutes. Then follow a variable rate of reinforcement until the completion of reading seatwork.

Example:

After Lester has worked for 8 minutes at his seatwork and making certain his behavior is appropriate, the teacher's aide pats him while observing his work. Later, after 7 minutes, the aide smiles at him while examining his work. After ten minutes the aide verbally praises Lester for working well. The schedule of reinforcement is as follows:

Reward	*Rate*
pat	8 minutes
smile	7 minutes
praise	10 minutes

By following a variable schedule of reinforcement the teacher is strengthening Lester's appropriate behavior during this segment of the school day. It is essential that reinforcement not be provided on schedule if at that moment the student is engaging in undesirable behavior since to do so would reward inappropriate behavior.

This example of a plan to improve Lester's in-class behavior is designed for use during reading instruction which represents only a small portion of his school day. It is assumed that the positive reinforcement that is carefully applied to Lester will result in a carry-over of desirable behavior to other segments of the school day but if transfer does not occur similar strategies should be applied during other portions of the day.

Transfer of appropriate responses to activities other than those occurring during reading instruction can be accelerated through teacher actions. As behavior is improved and desirable responses become more frequent under certain conditions, teachers can use similar reinforcers to improve behavior under similar but not identical conditions. Mrs. Crown could begin to apply a schedule of reinforcement to Lester during occasions in addition to those described above.

With some children, improved behavior during other segments of the school day will occur without a systematic plan of reinforcement. Often when the beginning of each day is carefully scheduled, children will gradually continue to respond favorably for increasingly longer time periods. The effect of this expansion is somewhat like a ripple because it results in a growing circle of positive behavior having as its core the original small portion of the school day that was so carefully planned.

Pair reinforcers with potential rewards / Pairing a reward with a potential reward is useful to teachers for purposes of changing student behavior and for facilitating issuance of rewards. Interest in new reinforcers often can be developed by pairing neutral and powerful events with strong reinforcers. In the aforementioned example, Lester was conditioned to view smiles and praise as rewarding. Conditioning was accomplished by a pairing technique. After additional rewards are developed, Mrs. Crown has more options available to her when responding to Lester. Pairing physical contact with a visual stimulus (smiling) and with an auditory stimulus (praise) develops easier means for issuing rewards. Physical contact requires close proximity, while other reinforcers permit control from a distance.

Pairing of rewards can be used to move preferences from primitive rewards, as represented by food and objects, to social rewards. For example:

> Richard has been conditioned to sit at his desk without disrupting the class by giving him a token for every 30 minutes of appropriate behavior. The teacher also places a star on Richard's chart, indicating that he has earned a token. Initially, stars were of neutral influence on his behavior but gradually he came to expect them in association with the tokens and viewed them as rewards. Then his teacher began to alternate stars with tokens as rewards and paired praise "very good" with rewards. Praise ultimately acquired the power of both reinforcers and was of sufficient influence to be used alone. The teacher, in this example, moved Richard from an object reward (tokens) to an interim reward (stars) and finally to a social reward "very good." The next step is to reduce gradually the use of praise leaving desired behavior as its own reward.

Pairing techniques permit many possibilities for developing additional reinforcers. For this reason, teachers should continually pair reinforcers with potential rewards so that students' repertories of reinforcers are enriched, making it possible to use many more events as rewards.

Use favorable conditions to shape behaviors / It is probably unreasonable for teachers to expect to identify those stimuli that favorably affect or have an adverse influence on student behavior. In most instances, it will be necessary to describe conditions under which students behave in certain ways. After these conditions are recognized by teachers, they can change behaviors by manipulating features of those settings in which undesirable responses occur. When favorable attributes of conditions are apparent to teachers, they can be used to shape responses toward desired behaviors.

In order to be aware of conditions with classrooms that are affecting student behavior, careful observations by teachers are essential. Environmental conditions that may influence student behavior consist of such elements as:

Time of day (mornings, afternoons, or hours)
Days of week
Areas of the classroom
Presence of certain individuals
Numbers of persons present
Type of subject matter being taught
Difficulty of subject matter

The example below describes how teacher observations and identification of positive features in the classroom can be used to modify student behavior.

Example:

Mrs. Brown observed that when she gave Marcia arithmetic assignments requiring no more than 15 minutes to complete and stayed near her, she completed the assignments quickly with few errors. But when Marcia was given assignments requiring more than 15 minutes to complete and consisting of problems equivalent in difficulty to those contained in shorter assignments, she worked only while Mrs. Brown was near her. Since Mrs. Brown did not stay near Marcia throughout the time she worked on longer assignments, she seldom completed these and made many errors on those which she did finish.

It appears that physical proximity of the teacher is reinforcing to Marcia. In this instance, Mrs. Brown paired her presence with verbal praise "keep up the good work Marcia." She began by giving arithmetic asignments to Marcia that could be completed within 10 minutes. Gradually assignments were made that required increasingly more time to complete. During arithmetic seatwork, Mrs. Brown systematically scheduled her presence near Marcia on a variable schedule of reinforcement and praised her for her efforts. Praise was also issued from afar in order to encourage Marcia to complete assignments. Because Mrs. Brown is observant, she is able to use those conditions that contribute to Marcia's desirable work habits.

Use successive steps in achieving outcomes. Teachers should bear in mind that short-term goals are more susceptible to reinforcement than are long-term goals. When behavioral outcomes are removed by several steps from the child's current functioning, it is important that each step is reinforced and that each is viewed as an outcome. In order to reinforce successive steps that progress toward a behavioral outcome, the task to be learned should be broken down into smaller components.

Example:

Scotty, a ten year old, is uncooperative when requested to perform certain academic tasks. Observations of his reactions to reading instruction are shown in Figure 6.3. His positive and negative reactions are summarized by two plus signs and one minus symbol. It should be pointed out that the word level of the story was two years below his demonstrated reading level (early 5th grade), otherwise, the example could lead one to infer incorrectly that the reading level of the story was too difficult for Scotty.

Recorded observations indicate that Scotty willingly listened to the story and behaved appropriately. He also engaged in a discussion concerning the story with his teacher. He was unwilling to read aloud, however, and when pressed to read he behaved undesirably by kicking and shouting. In other words, there are elements of reading instruction in which Scotty already participates without objection but oral reading, which is viewed by his teacher as important, is not willingly engaged in by Scotty. In order to change Scotty's responses when requested to read aloud certain procedures should be implemented by the teacher.

Mr. James, the teacher, should first establish the social learning task. It can be shown as:

Task	*Criterion*
Read aloud a story at an easy third grade level.	Reads the story aloud without objections.

He must then answer the question: which behaviors will progressively lead toward the fulfillment of this task? These behaviors are then viewed as short-term goals which will serve to meet the final outcome. Because criterion for completion of the task is specified in behavioral terms, Mr. James will know at which point Scotty has successfully completed the task.

A succession of tasks was devised for Scotty in order to encourage him to read orally. Note that at each point Scotty was reinforced. In this example, verbal praise ("Very good" and "That's fine") are used as rewards, while a wink is paired with these as a potential reward.

FIGURE 6.3. OBSERVATIONS OF SCOTTY'S REACTIONS TO READING
Reactions to Instructions

Child:	Scotty	Age:	10 - 2
Date:	November 15	Setting:	Resource Room
Observer:	Mr. James	Time of Day:	From 9:15 to 10:05

Reactions to Instruction

Activities		Reactions
Oral Reading: Scotty was asked to read a story that I read to him yesterday.	—	He said he didn't want to read, when I said: "I read to you yesterday. It's your turn today," he shouted "No" and began to kick the table.
Listening: I read a new story to him.	+	He became quiet and listened.
Discussion: Scotty talked about the story in response to my questions.	+	He accurately answered three questions about the story and was pleasant.

	Tasks	*Criteria*	*Rewards*	*Rate*
1,	listen to a story that is read.	listens without disruptive behavior	"very good" wink	at completion of task
2.	listen and hold book while story is read.	same as 1, plus holds book	"that's fine" wink	at completion of task

Tasks	Criteria	Rewards	Rate
3. same as 2, plus answers questions about the story.	same as 2, plus tries to answer questions	same as 2	at completion of task and after each answer
4. same as 3, plus locates answers to the question in the story; (after each paragraph a question will be asked).	same as 3, plus locates answers in the story	same as 3	at completion of task and after each answer
5. same as 3, plus locates and reads answers to the questions after each paragraph.	same as 3, plus locates and reads answers	"very good" wink	after reading correct answer
6. alternates with teacher in reading paragraphs of the story.	takes turn reading willingly	"that's fine" wink	after reading each selection
7. reads entire story aloud.	reads the story aloud without objections	wink "very good"	after every paragraph; midway through the story; and at completion

Task number 7 is the desired outcome and is arrived at by carefully reinforcing previous steps while gradually modifying demands of each succeeding task. Management strategy that was used in teaching each task will not be described here but some of the factors that Mr. James recognized as important are mentioned.

Scotty was given a choice of three books from which he was permitted to choose one. The books were written at a third grade reading level but the interest level was aimed at ten and eleven year old boys. Each text contained a series of stories that represented chapters involving the same main characters, making it easier for Scotty to recall names of leading characters and their experiences. The serial format helped to maintain his interest. Mr. James also used pictures in the text as "coming attractions" by encouraging Scotty to examine the pictures in the forthcoming story at the close of each session.

Each social learning task was designed to be achieved in one session if possible, although the sequence did not prevent devoting as many sessions as necessary until criterion for each task was met. In instances when criterion was not achieved, the subsequent session was devoted to that task. Scotty was expected to achieve a task only after the preceding one had been demonstrated. At completion of the sixth step, winking by Mr. James had acquired power as a reinforcer and was used as one in the final session.

Use prominent sense modes / Learning social responses, like learning academic skills, requires the use of sensory modalities. In order for a given stimulus to influence a student's behavior, the student must be aware of it. Children who are hindered by deficits in one or more senses will, by necessity, learn appropriate behavior less effectively through weaker channels than they will through their stronger sensory modes.

An assessment of sensory modalities of students will suggest which channels are most effectively used by them in responding to stimuli. This information can then be used by teachers in managing and improving behavior. Use of olfaction in social learning is perhaps the least obvious of the sensory channels that were discussed previously in this text. For that reason, the example below describes using the sense of smell in modifying behavior.

Example:

Jay is noted for kicking his teachers and anyone else who attempts to control his outbursts. He particularly dislikes being told to perform any academic tasks. When pressed to do so, he begins to curse and kick, striking any nearby shins. His academic skills are surprisingly good in view of his infrequent use of these skills due to his lack of cooperation and his placement in school on a half day basis.

It was noted, when assessing Jay's learning modalities, that his discrimination of odors was good. He responded positively to a cheap cologne and negatively to onion odor. Knowledge of what Jay con-

siders as representing pleasant and unpleasant odors permits rewarding desirable behavior and discouraging unwanted responses.

Jay's teacher, Mr. Page, arranged to have his aide assist Jay with
his arithmetic assignment in an area of the room away from other
children. The aide sprayed some of the cologne on her hands and
sprinkled a few drops on the paper containing arithmetic assignments.
By using pleasant odors in association with assignments, Mr. Page
was able to get Jay's cooperation and to develop more positive
responses.

An onion solution was available to be sprayed near Jay when he
kicked or cursed. Mr. Page informed him that the onion spray would
be used if he kicked others or cursed when told to do assignments. It
was necessary to use the repulsive odor on one occasion when Jay
kicked another student. His hands were immediately sprayed and Jay
discontinued kicking.

Weaken undesirable responses / Several effective techniques have
been used with children that result in a diminuition of inappropriate
behavior. While the emphasis in this text is on using rewards that
are viewed as positive or pleasant to recipients, at times using some
form of aversive conditioning becomes unavoidable.

Emission of an unpleasant odor in association with an undesirable
response is one way to try to extinguish inappropriate behavior.
There are however other techniques that are more feasible for use
with groups of children. These include removal of that which is
reinforcing unwanted responses; changing conditions under which
undesirable behavior occurs; and using aversive techniques.

Remove the reinforcement. If behavior is learned through reinforcement of that behavior, then withdrawal of the reward may
serve to extinguish responses. Removal of reinforcement may involve any one of several actions. It may simply require ignoring a
response, it may require withholding of a reward pending a change
in behavior, or a combination of both tactics may be necessary. The
example below deals with removal of reinforcement of inappropriate responses, withholding of reinforcement, and a combination
of the two in that order.

Example:

Jasper greets his teacher, Mr. Towne, with a slap on the back every
day as he enters his seventh period social studies class. Although he
dislikes this form of greeting, Mr. Towne had been replying with a
friendly "Hello, Jasper." After the greeting had been ignored two
consecutive days, Jasper discontinued the practice and went directly
to his seat.

On the third day, Mr. Towne smiled at Jasper after he was seated and said "Hi, Jasper."

Jasper resumed his original greeting on the fourth day but Mr. Towne ignored the behavior. When Jasper was seated, Mr. Towne smiled at him and greeted him in a friendly fashion. Jasper soon discontinued the undesirable behavior and went directly to his seat. Mr. Towne recognized the appropriate behavior from time to time, on what might be termed a variable rate of reinforcement.

Change the conditions. As was indicated earlier, it is often not clear what is the provoking stimulus but conditions under which certain responses occurred are readily observable. In such instances, a change in conditions may be warranted.

Changing conditions will also serve to weaken undesirable responses even when the stimulus that precipitated the misbehavior is evident. Teachers for example, rearrange classroom seating in an effort to render ineffective a provoking student. The two examples below describe changes in conditions, first when the stimulus is known and, in the second example, when the stimulus is not identifiable.

Example:

Harold responds to Mark's teasing by shouting and punching Mark. The teacher moved Mark to another area of the room, thus removing the provoking stimulus.

Michael becomes increasingly more unmanageable as the day increases. By 1:00 p.m., he refuses to participate in academic activities and when pressed to participate he screams. His teacher made arrangements through the principal to have Michael attend school mornings only. Gradually, his school day will be increased as his behavior improves.

Use aversive actions. At times when children misbehave repeatedly, teachers resort to punishment, ranging from mild rebukes to physical pain. Punishment is an aversive response to unacceptable behavior. There is a wide range of aversive possibilities. Jay's kicking was extinguished by using an odor that was repulsive to him which is a form of aversive conditioning. Typical aversive actions include removal from the group, confinement in an isolated setting, and verbal reprimands.

Events that are expected to be effective in weakening responses must be viewed as aversive by those children who are to be exposed to extinction procedures. If a teacher, for example, reprimands a student for misbehavior and it results in peer approval, it is unlikely that undesired behavior will be weakened if the student views peer approval as rewarding.

Punishment should be avoided by teachers whenever possible because it is likely to be issued in response to recent experiences which may be frustrating to the teacher. It is important that when punishment is issued that a fixed manner of presentation and criterion be established in advance.

Summary

Academic and social instruction represent two forms of educational treatment. Academic instruction is effective in improving learning through reinforcement techniques. These include specifying academic tasks; reinforcing correct responses; shaping responses; strengthening responses; and using observable outcomes.

It is essential that remedial instruction be used when students lack the prerequisites for learning certain skills. In order to be effective, teachers must be thoroughly familiar with the academic skill sequences and competent to assess academic functioning. Specific elements of academic skills should be taught using the child's best sensory mode.

Instruction of in-class behavior involves developing desirable responses through positive reinforcement and extinguishing undesirable responses. Social learning tasks should be divided into smaller steps in order to reward the achievement of each step. Additional rewards can be developed through pairing of reinforcers with potential rewards.

Unwanted behavior can be changed by altering conditions under which it occurs as well as by using aversive techniques.

Procedures for Evaluating Instruction

Changes in instructional tasks and **SEVEN**
strategies occur frequently in class-
rooms. Often new assignments are merely the result of students
completing a series of pages in workbooks and texts. Sometimes
teachers move to more difficult instruction on the basis of end of
unit tests or similar measures that are used to indicate that students
have mastered a given amount of content or skills.

Certainly a basis for change in instruction should be student performance. As student responses change, instruction too should
change. Results of evaluation can indicate when different instructional tasks are needed or when current tasks require continued
emphasis.

Evaluation is a process used to measure the relative effectiveness
of educational treatment (Good, 1959). In directive teaching, treatment is comprised of academic instruction and social instruction.

A standard is required for evaluative purposes in order to con-
trast actual performance with predetermined goals. Standards in
directive teaching are represented by terminal criteria that are set
in advance of treatment. Comparisons can then be made between
actual performance and expected performance (terminal criteria).

Results of these comparisons can be used for determining effects
of treatment and for making decisions with regard to subsequent

academic and social instruction. Using results derived from evaluations, teachers can decide such matters as which segments of
academic instruction require additional attention; which social responses need more or different reinforcement; and which of these
need changing or maintaining. Further instruction is then based,
in part, upon results of evaluation.

Features included in evaluating instruction as applied in directive
teaching are:

1) using repeated measures,
2) measuring gains under different conditions, and
3) measuring change over time.

These three elements of evaluation are presented in this chapter
followed by a brief discussion of ways to use results from evaluations. Finally, directive teaching is described within a computer
system.

USING REPEATED MEASURES

Each time results of teaching are compared with terminal criteria,
measuring takes place. Embedded into each teaching session is a
comparison of the results with terminal criteria. Since these comparisons are so frequent, they are termed here as *repeated measures*.
In order to measure the results of each session, it is necessary to
specify tasks and establish terminal criteria. When scores are needed
it becomes necessary also to quantify the results.

Specifying Tasks and Terminal Criteria

Let us say that Mrs. Smith has in her special class three boys who
require remedial instruction in reading skills. It is also difficult for
them to work in a group without becoming loud and fighting with
one another, resulting in classroom disruptions. She established the
academic and social learning tasks and terminal criteria as shown in
Figure 7.1.

Tasks in directive teaching as noted earlier are specific goals that
often require a series of teaching sessions. Steps that are taught
in achieving a goal are called sub-tasks. Just as each task has ter-

FIGURE 7.1. TASKS AND TERMINAL CRITERIA FOR THREE BOYS

Academic

Tasks	Criteria
1. Each boy reads and spells 30 one syllable words that begin with bl, cl, and br consonant blends:	1. Correctly reads and spells the thirty words.

block	clap	broke
black	clip	break
blast	clown	brim
blow	clam	brown
blank	class	brave
blare	clay	brag
blade	clean	brat
blame	clear	brace
blue	clerk	brake
blaze	cloth	brain

Social

2. Each boy works quietly with the other two and without disrupting other members of the class.	2. Works quietly during reading assignment and willingly shares materials with other two reading group members for ten (10) consecutive days.

minal criteria which serve to notify teachers when the task has been learned, each sub-task has associated with it evaluative criteria that serve the same function.

Teaching strategy (see Figure 5.2) is equivalent to a lesson plan and represents what is planned for one lesson that aims toward terminal criteria. Below are excerpts from the evaluation section of Mrs. Smith's teaching strategy form for Jack, Sam, and Art, the three boys for whom the academic and behavioral tasks were shown in Figure 7.1.

The first day Mrs. Smith taught these sub-tasks and measured their performance against these evaluative criteria for that day's lesson:

Sub-Tasks	Evaluative Criteria
1. recognition of: *block, blow, blast.*	1. reads *block, blast, blow* in sentences (3 pts.).
2. spelling of: *block, blow, blast.*	2. spells the three words in written form (3 pts.).
3. study the three words quietly as a group.	3. engages in a word card game without disrupting others (1 pt.).

Results of Mrs. Smith's measurement for each criterion are shown in that same order below:

1. Jack met the criteria for this task. Sam read *blast* and *blow*, while Art read *block*.
2. Jack correctly spelled all three words. Sam correctly spelled *blast* and *blow*. Art correctly spelled *block*.
3. While playing the card game, they began arguing among themselves but they did not become loud and did not disrupt others.

Quantifying Results

Scores provide a quick and convenient way to compare two or more performances of the same individual. They also permit ready comparisons among individuals. Scores can be developed by placing a numerical value on each segment of a sub-task. Note that each sub-task above is weighted. Since each portion of a task is weighted by one point, we have assumed that each response is of equal value.

Number one provides a total of three points; number two, three points; and number three, one point. In this example, each word in sub-tasks one and two represents a point, while sub-task three when performed correctly allows for one point. Terminal criteria for sub-task three could also have been devised so as to allow students to earn points based on the length of time they refrained from disrupting others.

When results of learning are quantified, data are amenable to a variety of manipulations and permit calculating averages, gain scores, and other statistics. While these calculations provide valuable data for comparisons and research, they are at least one step removed from actual responses. In other words, some value for teaching is lost when performance is quantified.

Result of the three boys' performances on the sub-tasks listed above were quantified and are reflected in figure 7.2.

FIGURE 7.2.   RESULTS OF INSTRUCTION FOR THREE BOYS

Sub-Tasks	One	Two	Three	Total Score	Possible Score	Percent Correct
Art	1	1	1	3	7	43
Jack	3	3	1	7	7	100
Sam	2	2	1	5	7	71

Built into each teaching session is a measure of progress made by students. In every teaching session, teachers should include evaluative criteria as measures of student progress. These results are then used to devise subsequent sub-tasks.

Mrs. Smith established the following sub-tasks and measurement criteria for the three boys.

Sub-task 1:

Jack — recognition of: *block, blast, blow, black, clap, clip*
Art and Sam — recognition of: *blast, blow, block*

Criteria for measurement of sub-task 1:

Jack — reads the six words correctly in sentences (6 points)
Art and Sam—read the three words correctly in sentences (3 points)

Sub-task 2:

Jack — writes the six words correctly
Art and Sam — write the three words correctly

Criteria for measurement of sub-task 2:

Jack — writes the six words when presented auditorally (6 points)
Art and Sam — write the three words when presented auditorally (3 points)

Sub-task 3:

Jack, Art, and Sam — work together without disruption of the class and without arguing among themselves.

Criteria for measurement of sub-task 3:

Jack, Art, and Sam — play "word card game" without disrupting others (1 point) and without arguing with each other (1 point). The results of the boys' performances on the three sub-tasks are:

Sub-task 1:

Jack — 6 points — read all six sentences correctly
Art — 3 points — read the three sentences correctly
Sam — 3 points — read the three sentences correctly

Sub-task 2:

> Jack — 5 points — incorrectly spelled *black*
> Art — 3 points — correctly spelled the three words
> Sam — 3 points — correctly spelled the three words

Sub-task 3:

> Jack — 1 point — did not disrupt class but argued with Sam during card game.
> Sam — 0 points — disrupted class. Loudly argued with Jack.
> Art — 2 points —did not disrupt class and did not argue with Sam and Jack.

Following instruction of these three sub-tasks, Mrs. Smith will have acquired additional measures of the progress toward mastery of the original tasks made by these students. With each succeeding session, she can continue to accumulate data in narrative and numerical forms.

Purposes of Repeated Measurements

Measurement during each segment of instruction provides valuable information to the teacher. Results form a basis for teachers to make at least five important decisions about teaching and managing children. These five points are discussed below.

1. *Results of repeated measurements indicate the effectiveness of a particular treatment.* If instruction is of sufficient value it should result in a change in performance. In the preceding description it seems reasonable to credit instruction that was used with Art as being effective. After the first treatment, he received a total of 3 points out of a possible 7 points. He received a score of 8 points out of a possible 8 points following the second session.

These results can be viewed in several ways with respect to treatment. One view is to conclude that the reinforcement used in conjunction with the sub-tasks was very effective in improving Art's responses. It is seen in the over-all effect of the treatment; he gained 58 percent between the first treatment and the second as shown in Figure 7.3. This gain is even more impressive in view of the fact that an additional requirement was added to sub-task 3 for the second session (study with the other two boys without argument).

The effectiveness of teaching can also be judged. Note that Art was the only one of three boys that met the two point criterion for sub-task three. Even with the adverse modeling and peer pressure

FIGURE 7.3. GAIN SCORES FOLLOWING TWO INSTRUCTIONAL SESSIONS FOR THREE BOYS

Sessions	One Criteria		Two Criteria		Differences	
	Score	Percent	Score	Percent	Score	Percent
Art	3/7	43	8/8	100	5	57
Jack	7/7	100	12/13	92	*	*
Sam	5/7	71	6/8	75	1	4

*Sub-tasks were changed for second session

that inevitably occurs in a small group, Art neither argued with Sam and Jack or disrupted others. We can infer that the treatment used in teaching sub-task three to Jack had a positive effect on his performance.

It should be noted that because Jack reached criteria during the first session new sub-tasks were taught to him in the second session. He was, therefore, expected to learn additional sub-tasks because of his rapid achievement in the first session.

2. *Results of measurements in narrative form indicate the specific gains that have occurred.* Numbers are a convenient form for analyzing effects of treatment, but, as was noted above, the use of numbers tends to obscure instructional value of an evaluation for individual children. To know that a child missed five out of ten arithmetic problems does convey to a teacher that the child answered 50 percent of the problems accurately. Additional information would be more valuable for further teaching. It would be helpful for teachers to know which problems representing certain arithmetical processes were passed and missed. This type of information (i.e., 2 three-place subtraction problems and 3 two-place multiplication problems were missed) would suggest to teachers which processes should be retaught. It would also suggest when alternate instructional procedures must be used with students.

The teacher would be well informed with such specific information about students' achievement. Built-in criteria for evaluative purposes allow teachers to compare learners' responses from one session to the next. Inconsistent performance, where a child responds incorrectly the second day to a task that he passed previously, can be readily noted and programmed into subsequent teaching.

3. *Results of measurements suggest the point at which instruction should begin.* Repeated measurements permit teachers to acquire information about children's responses that assists in deciding what needs to be retaught, what was learned, and what is reasonable to reach next.

Results of Mrs. Smith's measurement for each criterion in the first teaching session are more meaningful for teaching purposes before being transformed into numerical form. By knowing, for example, that Sam recognized the words *blast* and *blow* in meeting criteria for the first sub-task, Mrs. Smith had a sound basis for an instructional decision. She could choose to teach other words that begin with the *bl* consonant blend, building on that which was just learned, or she could decide, as she did, to repeat the systematic instruction of the same words until all three words are mastered.

In the academic skill areas such as reading and arithmetic, sequence of skill development often requires that prerequisites to higher level skills be known prior to learning more difficult skills. Consequently, repeated measurements serve to inform teachers about which skills can be taught with the reasonable assurance that they can be readily learned.

Social responses, also, tend to follow a sequence of development. Children must have acquired certain responses in order for larger more complicated behavior to be developed. Attending behavior is a clear example. Those who have yet to develop attention toward academic tasks of short durations typically will have trouble attending to similar tasks for longer periods of time. Similarly, the child who is unaccustomed to cooperative activities with his classmates will be unwilling to share during group activities.

4. *Results indicate when teachers can move learners toward mastery of other tasks or sub-tasks.* When students have met terminal criteria for a task, teachers then have a basis for deciding that another task can be established and taught.

Mrs. Smith changed the demands for two sub-tasks for Jack because he moved closer to achievement of the academic task. He read three words as required in the first sub-task and he correctly spelled the same words in meeting criteria for sub-task number two. As a consequence of Jack's performance she added an additional word to the instructional tasks that begins with a *bl* (black) and introduced two words that contain the initial *cl* consonant blend. She continued to include three original words for added practice and as a way to incorporate successful performance as a potential reward for Jack.

Four teaching sessions later we find that Jack has satisfied all requirements for those academic and behavioral tasks. That is, he learned to read and to spell correctly all words shown in Figure 7.1 which satisfies criteria for Task 1. He also mastered Task 2 by quietly doing reading assignments and working cooperatively with Art and Sam. At this juncture, Mrs. Smith will make a decision concerning Jack. Some options facing her include: a) She can continue to expose Jack to instructions for achievement of the two tasks to give him more practice since Art and Sam have not yet fulfilled these task requirements. b) She can devise new reading and social tasks for Jack and place him in another instructional group. c) Or, she could implement both of the aforementioned options.

5. *Results of measurements established a basis for subsequent instruction.* Not only do results of evaluation indicate that the students can move to the next instructional step as indicated in number four, but they also give clues as to what the next step can be.

For example, Mrs. Smith believes that Jack can begin to learn and apply rules of syllabication which, if mastered, will permit him to attack unfamiliar words and thus become an independent reader. The basis for her belief that Jack could learn to generalize phonic principles was his quick grasp of the notion that those words in the list that end in silent e were preceded by a long vowel. Therefore, Jack was placed in a newly organized reading group for the purpose of applying three rules of syllabication. These are:

a) If there are two vowel letters together in a word, usually the first stands for a long vowel and the second is silent.
b) If there is one vowel letter in a word it usually represents a short vowel sound unless it is at the end of the word.
c) If there are two vowel letters in a word, one of which is final e, the first represents a long vowel sound and the final e is silent.

The procedures used by Mrs. Smith for the newly constituted group will be the same as other directive teaching procedures.

MEASURING GAINS UNDER DIFFERENT CONDITIONS

One sign of effective learning is seen when what has been learned under one set of conditions is applied appropriately under different conditions. This carry-over is commonly referred to as *transfer of learning* (Thorndike, 1924). E. L. Thorndike long ago demonstrated the fallacies associated with training in formal disciplines as an attempt to improve thinking abilities. His studies clearly indicated that generalizing of learning is not easily accomplished. For transfer of learning to occur readily, instruction should be directly related to the information, skills, or circumstances of the new learning.

Evaluating Transfer of Learning

Observations under dissimilar conditions will reveal if learned responses are being transferred. Teachers can determine if responses that have been learned under one set of conditions are being transferred to other conditions by sampling students' performances under different conditions.

Procedures for evaluating responses under different conditions are essentially the same as other evaluative procedures previously described. For example, Mrs. Smith wanted to determine if Jack transfers his cooperative behavior to others. In order to evaluate this, she placed him in another special group for the purpose of teaching rules of syllabication.

The other three members of the reading group are not noted for being disruptive in class but tend to be uncooperative toward one another. Tasks and terminal criteria for the group are shown in Figure 7.4.

FIGURE 7.4.   TASKS AND TERMINAL CRITERIA FROM A DIRECTIVE TEACHING PLAN

Students: Jack, Harold, Martha, Robert

Teacher: Mrs. Smith

Time of Day: 9:15 - 9:30

Academic

Tasks	*Terminal Criteria*
1. Learn three rules of sylla-bication:	1. Apply each rule by:
a) two vowel letters to-gether	a) pronouncing correctly 5 words per rule (15 pts.)
b) one vowel letter in a word	b) citing each rule and providing 2 examples (6 pts.)
c) two vowel letters, one is silent e	

Social

1. Works cooperatively with all group members

2. Cooperative activities will not disrupt other class members

1. Willingly shares materials with all members (3 pts.)

2. Works quietly (1 pt.)

Mrs. Smith can observe Jack's performance on two social tasks to determine if he does apply learned responses (cooperation) under different conditions. Those conditions to be taken into account are:

1. *Differences in task requirements.* Social tasks are being held constant since in both plans they are identical, but the academic tasks are different.

Characteristics of tasks can serve to facilitate or inhibit transfer of learning to other settings. Those characteristics that represent similarities of tasks will in some instances assist in successfully completing the new tasks. In other instances, similarities will interfere with learning. In general those characteristics that tend to confuse learners will make transfer difficult, while those similarities that aid in mastery of a new task make transfer of learning easier.

For example, applying those reading skills that were acquired through classroom instruction to newspaper reading at home requires little if any readjustment. Similarities of the two tasks will facilitate transfer. On the other hand, applying the same reading skills to reading aloud before an audience requires a number of changes. Reading well aloud requires correct pronunciations, self confidence, and clear speaking. None of these is essential for silent reading in the classroom. Differences in the two task requirements do not necessarily interfere with performance of either task and to some extent may serve to facilitate mastery of both.

2. *Differences in time of day.* This variable will be held constant. Jack's former group was taught from 9:15 to 9:30 the same time of day as is the newly constituted group.

Importance of time of day as a variable relates to attributes of the learner which could change and affect his performance. His bodily condition could change and interfere with meeting task demands. Fatigue is one factor that is often associated with time of day. Many children who present learning and behavioral problems function differently early in the school day than they do later that same day. Nearness to meal time is another consideration. Instruction that occurs immediately before lunch may be responded to differently than that which takes place just after lunch.

Illness is not necessarily associated with the variable "time of day," but it is a factor that influences the child's functioning across all variables. For example, Jack may have a head cold and is too uncomfortable to be cooperative in the reading group.

3. *Differences in group members.* This variable has been changed purposely in order to determine if Jack transfers learned behavior from one group to another.

Social behavior is affected by a change in conditions. While Jack may have learned to work well with Art and Sam in the classroom, he may continue to behave inappropriately in the classroom toward other children. He may also find it more difficult to engage in other activities cooperatively with Art and Sam.

4. *Difference in reinforcement.* Type of rewards and schedule of reinforcement constitute other important variables. Possibly the reward for desired performance has diminished in effectiveness. Praise, for example, may be so frequent that it has become a routine matter and has lost its power of reinforcement. In such instances, it may be necessary to change rate of reinforcement or to use a different reward.

Mrs. Smith intends to use the same reward (praise and group recognition) for Jack. She will continue to issue reinforcement at the close of each session.

Ways to Facilitate Transfer

When observations under dissimilar conditions reveal that learned responses are not being applied across different conditions, the teacher should utilize directive teaching procedures under different conditions in order to teach desired responses. At first, some aspects of conditions under which desired responses occur should be used to help facilitate transfer. The following example will serve to show how children can be taught to transfer social responses from one setting to another.

Example:

> Jack, Art, and Sam now work cooperatively in small group activities without disrupting other children. It has been observed that they behave appropriately toward each other on the playground, indicating that their learned responses have been transferred to another setting. However, the three boys have difficulty working cooperatively with others in the classroom and playing with other children.

Mrs. Smith began teaching the social task of working appropriately with others by gradually including additional children in the small group. First she placed Howard in the group with the three boys. Later she added two other boys. After they worked well together, she assigned a task that involved play activities. As the boys increased their social competencies, they were assigned more tasks that required involvement with other children. This procedure continued until Jack, Art, and Sam had successfully worked and played with all other members of the special class.

Confusion of academic instruction can be avoided by teaching closely related responses in different contexts. Teachers should call to the attention of students similarities and differences and should give clues to aid students in recall of learning.

Tasks that are similar, when taught in close proximity to each other, tend to confuse students and do interfere with learning particularly when teachers fail to point out similarities and differences to learners.

Word study is an example of the type of instructional content that can be confusing to students. For instance, teaching spelling of *desert* and *dessert* when taught in the same session could be confusing if not carefully presented. Even though meanings of the two words are greatly different their spellings are almost identical. If spellings alone are emphasized rather than meanings, inaccurate recall in written form could be the result.

MEASUREMENTS OVER TIME

Maintenance and use of what was learned at an earlier time is another sign of effective learning. Commonly noted is the observation that frequently used responses tend to be maintained for longer periods of time than do responses that are seldom used. Using social or academic responses at varying intervals serves to reinforce them on an intermittent schedule of reinforcement. Results of these responses provide feedback to the individuals as to the appropriateness of their use. Thus, learners are provided bases for adjusting their responses as they are strengthened through use.

Many academic and behavioral skills are maintained naturally because they are used by necessity in school and in other related activities. Sometimes they are sustained through using higher order responses that require use of or understanding of more fundamental concepts. For example, using multiplication facts is inherent in calculating problems in division. Similarly, attending behavior is continued and developed as requirements in school demand an increased amount of attention.

Those responses that are not reinforced either as a matter of course or systematically by others will tend to be less evident and may be extinguished through disuse. If teachers wish to maintain what has been learned, they must make certain that opportunities for its use are available to students.

Observations over a period of time will reveal if learning has been maintained. These observations are represented by measures which are a part of an evaluation program. Measurements can be applied following learning after a short lapse of time or over longer intervals of time. Each is discussed below.

Short Term Evaluation

Evaluation that is a part of each instructional session, as described previously, is one type of short term measurement. When instruction is completed, student performance is compared immediately with the previously specified terminal criteria. This point of immediate comparison extending across time to five days is designated herein as *short term evaluation.*

One question to be answered in an evaluation of past learnings is: *At what level has the learning been maintained?* Answers to this question indicate if reteaching is needed. The teacher may present an assignment equivalent to or identical to what was learned earlier and apply the terminal criteria that were used previously. Results will indicate if learning was maintained and at what level. In addition, periodic evaluations of past learning provide reinforcement of that learning and thus helps to maintain responses.

Example:

Three days after Jack, Sam and Art had met terminal criteria for spelling these words: *block, blow, blast,* Mrs. Smith evaluated their recall for spelling the three words. She included them in a test containing words that were learned more recently. All there words were written correctly by each student.

Long Term Evaluation

Evaluation that occurs at least six days after tasks were initially mastered is considered to be long term. Let us say, for example, that Art was absent from school for five days. Before resuming instruction, Mrs. Smith wants to determine whether what Art had learned his last day in school had been retained. She simply uses the teaching strategy that was used on that day in the desired instruction. Current results are then compared with previous performance. Comparisons will indicate to the teacher if: a) Art met the terminal criteria; b) his performance was below or above his previous achievement; c) additional instruction is required.

Long term evaluation may be useful for other reasons as well as for determining the effects of absence from school. It is helpful prior to placement in another class such as re-entry into a regular classroom. In such instances, results can be used to determine if the student has the necessary skills to be successful in another placement and to suggest which skills need additional instruction.

By maintaining a file of prior directive teaching plans and teaching strategy forms for each child, teachers can readily engage in short and long term evaluation when desired. The file can also serve as a valuable resource to use with other children who are in need of similar instruction.

Uses of Evaluative Results

Descriptive information forms a basis for identifying and selecting tasks and teaching strategies. If instruction has been effective, a change in performance of the student will be evident. Such a change would automatically result in a change in descriptive information, which in turn will contribute to the establishment of new tasks and different instructional treatment.

Change in Descriptive Information

Note the change in social behavior among Jack, Art, and Sam in the earlier example concerning their cooperative working habits. As their behavior while working in small groups improved, a change in their functioning occurred. The academic task shown in Figure 7.1, when mastered, resulted in a significant change in descriptive information. When the criteria were met by the three boys, they were reading stories independently and writing short sentences. Successful completion of the social task in Figure 7.1 saw them cooperating in group activities. This change in functioning permitted them to engage in other activities as a group and to function more appropriately with others.

Change in Treatment

Change in functioning may suggest a different treatment. Improved performance in learning a particular type of response might result in using more effectively sensory-expressive modalities. For example, an initial assessment suggested that Howard should be taught reading word recognition by pairing auditory discrimination, his strong channel, with visual discrimination, his weaker modality. At the end of several months of such instruction, Howard demonstrated sufficient improvement in utilizing his vision for reading. It was then possible to rely more on vision and less on auditory learning in reading instruction.

Similar changes in reinforcement contribute to a change in teaching strategy. When a student's preference for rewards changes even though the conditions are similar to those under which he first revealed his preference, the use of different reinforcers is indicated. When the rate of a desired response is to the point of diminution, a different schedule of reinforcement may be necessary.

Change in Tasks

When students achieve the terminal criteria for a task, their achievement indicates that the task can be changed. Other tasks are then established based on descriptive information which was influenced by mastery of prior learnings. If a change in performance is not evident, the tasks have not been learned. Persistent failure to master tasks suggest to teachers a need to change either tasks, terminal criteria, or strategy.

A change in task should be based upon the curriculum, or instructional goals for students and the prerequisite skills evidenced by students (Glaser, 1966). Thus when students have mastered tasks, if they are hierarchal in nature, the next level of task in the series may be taught. Or if it is one of a series of related but nonsequential tasks, another task in the series may be selected for instruction. When students fail to master tasks following a reasonable amount of instruction, teachers should consider those prerequisite skills needed for mastery of the task. By changing the task to a lower order, it may be possible to teach missing prerequisite responses, which will in turn ready learners for more difficult tasks, as well as permit using success on easier tasks as reinforcement.

A change in terminal criteria would result in lowering the task requirements. Thus, a student who was expected to master 10 successive trials of a new response but failed to emit more than 8 consecutive correct responses could reach criterion if the teacher designated the lower number as mastery. The same task could be included in subsequent instruction in order to maintain and improve student performance.

Changing strategy could include modifications to types and schedules of reinforcement or changes in the instructional materials and sensory modalities that are used for receiving particular instruction.

Using Computer Assistance

Procedures used in directive teaching require considerable teacher time and effort. Specifying tasks, terminal criteria, and instructional strategies demand a change in function for many teachers in addition to their acquiring new instructional skills.

A reduction in time and effort can result from using computers to assist teachers. The system described below is based upon a model that has evaluation as an integral part. It consists of two interrelated sections.

Observations of Students

The first component contains dependent variables, representing information that was obtained on each student through assessment techniques as described in Chapter 4. These variables are shown in

FIGURE 7.5.   OBSERVATIONS OF STUDENTS

Behavior	Reinforcement	Modes
Academic Responses	Types	Visual Haptics
Social Responses	Rates	Auditory Olfactory

Figure 7.5 as observations of students. Areas of student behavior that should be assessed include:

1. Academic and social responses. These are responses to academic instruction including attending behavior, academic skill functioning, and responses toward instructional material and assignments. Social responses are a result of interactions toward teachers and peers.

2. Reinforcement. This category is represented by types of rewards; primary, interim, social, and schedules of rewards needed to maintain the desired responses.

3. Modes. These are the sensory modalities through which students demonstrate accurate expressions of learning specific responses.

Information representing observations of students can be presented to a computerized program in order to obtain instructional strategies for teaching students.

Instructional Strategies

The second component of this system contains independent variables that are manipulated in an effort to achieve desired outcomes.

FIGURE 7.6. INSTRUCTIONAL STRATEGIES

Tasks	Reinforcement	Modes
Academic	Types	Visual Haptics
Social	Schedules	Auditory Olfactory

These variables are shown in Figure 7.6. The major elements of instructional strategies include:

1. Tasks. These tasks consist of academic and social responses including academic skills such as arithmetic, reading, and spelling. Attending behavior and interactions with others are also subsumed under the category entitled "tasks." Specific tasks are stored in an information retrival system ready to be selected when the academic and social responses are presented (Sutherland, 1966).

2. Reinforcement. Stored also in the information bank are various types and schedules of reinforcement. The appropriate ones are selected and printed on the instructional strategy form based on the assessment information concerning students' rates and types of reinforcement.

3. Modes. Those sensory modalities appropriate for teaching selected tasks coupled with the student's demonstrated facility for learning through particular modes are indicated in the instructional strategy.

The computer produces a printed instructional plan based on observational information. This plan indicates strategies for achieving particular outcomes. It also provides a format that permits teachers to report results of instruction (evaluation). In turn, these results are presented to the computer for additional strategies.

Computerized Instructional Strategies / If a wide variety of instructional strategies are readily available in a computerized system, the assessment information can be fed into the computerized retrival system. By matching present responses an instructional plan can be produced. The strategy should indicate instructional materials to be used showing pages and items. It should also include tasks, terminal criteria, and type and schedules of reinforcement.

FIGURE 7.7.   SIMULATED INSTRUCTIONAL STRATEGY PRINT-OUT

Sub-tasks

4   reads and spells: clap, clip, class, click, clock, clop, club, cluck, clutch

Criteria: reads in sentences — 9
             writes words when dictated in sentences — 9

R:	Type	Rate	Paired	Rate
	Praise	E-S	K-P	C

Modes: A-V

Materials:
     4.79 — 1 2 3 4 5 6 7 8 9
     4.80 — A
     4.81 — A
     4.82 — A
     12.9 — 6 7 8

     Language Master

Evaluation:

     Criteria passed

R:	Type	Rate	Paired	Rate

Materials:

Modes:

The simulated print-out in Figure 7.7 shows a sub-task to be taught to Art, Jack, and Sam. Also included are terminal criteria for measuring mastery of sub-task number four. Because the criteria are quantified, the teacher, Mrs. Smith, can relate criteria to evaluation in quantified form as well as in descriptive form. The evaluation section is completed by Mrs. Smith after instruction for presentation to the computer so that another strategy format can be printed.

Available instructional materials are coded. Digits to the left of the decimal refer to texts or workbooks. Numbers to the right of the decimal are pages, and figures to the right of the dash represent items on those pages relevant to the tasks. For example in Figure 7.7, the first two lines of materials are read as follows:

1. Textbook four, page 79, items one through nine relate to the sub-task.
2. All items on page 80 of textbook four are relevant to the sub-task.

The last line under materials indicates that the Language Master would also be a suitable tool to use in this instance.

Reinforcement is indicated by R suggesting that verbal praise (very good) should be issued at end of session (E-S). The reinforcement is to be paired with a potential reward, knowledge of performance (K-P), after every response.

Modalities for presenting instruction should be auditory simultaneous with visual stimuli. The Language Master is particularly well suited for a simultaneous presentation because it voices the word sound as the word is displayed. Textbook four[1] also lends itself to using auditory and visual modes because its format readily permits word study by a group.

Strategies can be provided without using retrieval mechanisms, as was noted earlier in this book, but considerably more time and effort are required. Initially it will be necessary to write strategies for computer programs. As these are placed in data retrieval systems, they can become a part of a permanent storage for use upon demand.

Evaluation is clearly related to a computerized system. As the teacher compares student performance with terminal criteria and indicates results, changes in strategy will be selected by the computer and incorporated into the next print-out. Consequently, the computer assists teachers in writing strategies and individualizing instruction.

---

[1] Charles C. Fries, Rosemary G. Wilson, and Mildred K. Rudolph, Merrill Linguistic Readers (Columbus, Ohio: Charles E. Merrill Publishing Co., 1966).

Summary

Evaluation in directive teaching provides teachers with information concerning the effects of their instruction. This information is then used for determining which segments of academic material and behavioral skills need to be retaught and if students have acquired prerequisite skills for more difficult tasks.

Evaluative criteria can be quantified so that results are amenable to statistical analysis. Although results in descriptive form are more desirable for purposes of instruction.

Evaluation is also useful for assessing if students transfer learning to conditions other than those under which learning initially occurred. These conditions include maintenance of learning over periods of time as well as application in different contexts.

By using computer assistance, teachers can reduce time needed for strategy writing while continuing to individualize instruction. A computerized program contains all elements needed for devising instructional strategies. These are selected electronically when the computer is presented with assessments of students. As evaluative information concerning students' performance is presented, changes in strategy reflect evaluation results.

Glossary

Important terms and phrases used in this book are defined below. This glossary includes both technical terms and common words used in a special or restricted sense in psychology and education. In each case, the meaning given is that used or implied in the book. For additional meanings and more complete definitions, see Horace B. English and Ava C. English, *A Comprehensive Dictionary of Psychological and Psychoanalytical Terms*. New York: Longmans, Green and Co., 1958. For additional definitions of educational terms see Carter V. Good, *Dictionary of Education*. New York: McGraw-Hill Book Company, 1959.

Academic Learning Task: a required act, the mastery of which results in acquiring subject matter and is reflected in a change in responses (behavior).

Academically Handicapped Children: children demonstrating significant discrepancies between their functional intelligence and their academic achievement, poor quality of achievement is common. These children often show no progress following standard academic instruction.

Anticipated Achievement: predicted accomplishment using a test of intelligence as a criterion measure.

Anticipatory Statement: a forewarning by teachers prior to events. These provide students with time to change the pace of their current activities and to get set for a change in behavior.

Assessment: a survey of student functioning to determine those responses and skills that are adequate and those yet to be learned or mastered.

Associative Learning: a systematic pairing of a powerful reward or event with an event or response not fully developed. See Pairing.

Attending Behavior: student responses to relevant stimuli.

Auditory Learning: discrimination and recall using hearing as the sensory mode.

Auditory Stimuli: stimuli associated with auditory sensory processes, e.g. change in voice used to signal a new activity.

Auto-instructional Materials: designed to provide immediate feedback to learners about the accuracy of their responses, e.g. programmed instruction.

Aversive Conditioning: an attempt to change behavior by being punitive. See Negative Reinforcement.

Avoidance Technique: preventing disruptive behavior by anticipating difficulties. See Anticipatory Statement.

Behavioral Modeling: learning through observing and imitating others.

Behavioral Task: a required act that when mastered results in a change in responses. Included are: 1) academic learning tasks, and 2) social learning tasks.

Behaviorally Handicapped Children: those whose responses interfere with adjustment to school. Includes children whose rate of behavior interferes with learning, and those whose weak control of behavior interferes with learning.

Computerized Instructional Strategy: an instructional plan developed by matching assessment information with instructional plans derived from a computerized retrieval system.

Contingency Management: a technique for obtaining desired behavior by informing students which behaviors will be rewarded in advance.

Continuous Schedule: pattern of reinforcement, when reinforcement occurs each time a desired response is emitted.

Contrived Task Approach: a technique used to assess reinforcement in relation to instruction.

Criterion Level: predetermined standard of acceptable performance.

Criterion-Level Test: a test that shows whether objectives of a lesson have been met and where further instruction is needed.

Cueing: the use of signals to elicit desired responses.

Delayed Recall: recollection of learned material after a lapse of time.

Dependent Variable: student behavior that is amenable to change through instructional treatment.

Depth Psychology: doctrines postulating that children with adjustment or learning problems are evidencing symptoms of deep seated neuroses.

Directive Teaching: a system that enables teachers to be effective in academic instruction while simultaneously responding to student's social behavior. It consists of: 1) gathering descriptions of behavior, 2) using this information for planning instructional strategies, 3) simultaneous application and evaluation.

Discrimination: detection of differences through one or more senses.

Educational Diagnosis: classifying students on the basis of educationally relevant information.

Embedded Methodology: methods of presentation that are built into instructional media, e.g. programmed texts.

Evaluation: procedure used to measure the effects of an instructional treatment.

Expression: any observable response.

Expressive Modes: any observable response involving one or combination of several sensory channels.

External Reward: any visible reinforcement.

Fixed-Interval Schedule: pattern of reinforcement, when reward occurs at specified time intervals.

Fixed-Ratio Schedule: pattern of reinforcement, when reward occurs after a specific number of correct responses.

Forced-Choice Preference Schedule: an interview schedule requiring students to select one of a pair of potential rewards.

Handicap: burdens imposed on the learner that cannot be resolved due to body dysfunction or impairment.

Haptics: discrimination through the sense of touch.

Immediate Recall: instant recollection of stimuli presented moments before recall.

Independent Variable: instructional treatment.

Informal Testing Techniques: teacher observation, teacher-made tests, and interviews.

Instructional Reading Level: reading level of a student that requires some teacher assistance.

Interim Reward: symbols and objects that represent something of value to an individual.

Intermittent Schedule: pattern of reinforcement, when reward is based on irregular intervals.

Internal Reinforcement: intrinsic satisfaction to learners.

Law of Effect: a principle indicating that any response which results in satisfaction to the individual is likely to be repeated.

Learning Handicapped Children: pupils who have either serious academic learning deficiencies or serious social learning problems or both. These problems are evidenced by maladjustment in school.

Long-term Evaluation: measurement of student performance at least six days after initial mastery of tasks.

Negative Reinforcement: dissatisfaction to the learner following a response, e.g. punishment.

Observable Outcomes: evident effects of instruction.

Observational Techniques: noting student responses under specified conditions.

Olfactory Learning: discrimination and recall using smell as the sensory mode.

Operant Behavior: behavior for which the specific eliciting stimulus is unknown.

Operant Conditioning: systematic application of behavioral management procedures in which responses emitted by children are shaped.

Overachievement: when an individual's achievement exceeds his anticipated achievement. A result of measurement error.

Over-Emittors of Behavior: children described as restless, attention-seeking, disruptive, boisterous, hyperactive, overly aggressive, and unruly. Those who over-respond.

Pairing: associating a pleasant event with an activity of neutral value. A method for developing rewards.

Participating Behavior: student responses that involve interactions with others.

Positive Reinforcement: a response followed by an event that results in reducing a need and is satisfying to the student. Also termed rewards or reinforcers.

Potential Reward: a neutral event or stimulus that becomes reinforcing as a result of being paired with a pleasant event.

Pre-requisites to Learning: competencies needed to learn a task.

Primitive Rewards: edibles used as reinforcers. Same as Primary Rewards.

Programmed Instruction: sequential programs designed for independent study that provide immediate feedback to learners. See Auto-Instructional Materials.

Prompting Technique: used to involve reluctant students in learning situations by providing enough information to guarantee correct responses. See Cueing.

Receptive-Expressive Modes: channels used by humans for receiving stimuli and responding. Same as sensory-expressive modes.

Remedial Instruction: teaching reserved for children who are severely handicapped in achieving basic skills and who are in need of individualized instruction.

Repeated Measures: comparisons of student responses with criteria during each teaching session.

Resource Room: a classroom containing materials, equipment and a qualified teacher who instructs handicapped children on a scheduled basis.

Response Repertoire: responses that are within the capacity of a student.

Reward Options: available choices of reinforcement for a given student.

Reward System: reinforcement scheme composed of rewards preferred by students and rate of presentation.

Secondary Rewards: reinforcement acquired through associating primary rewards with other events usually social in character.

Sensory Modes: channels of the human organism used to receive stimuli.

Shaping: presenting clues that guide responses toward mastery of a task. See Succesive Approximations.

Short-Term Evaluation: immediate comparison of student performance with previously specified terminal criteria. Comparison extending across time to five days.

Social Learning Task: a required act, the mastery of which results in a change in social behavior in school.

Social Reward: secondary reinforcement involving social recognition.

Stimulus-Response: behavior exhibited as a result of differential teacher or environmental stimuli.

Sub-Task: a step in a series leading to or comprising a task.

Successive Approximations: a series of responses each more closely approaching the desired behavior. See Shaping.

Teaching Strategy: a plan that details which students will be taught, what they will be taught, and how they will be taught in order to achieve specified behavioral tasks.

Terminal Criteria: standards of acceptable performance indicating mastery of tasks. Includes desired behavior and the conditions under which it must occur. Terminal criteria are established prior to instruction.

Transfer of Learning: carry-over of what has been learned under one set of conditions and applied appropriately under different conditions.

Underachievement: a significant difference between expected achievement and actual achievement, with lower performance in the latter.

Underachiever: one who performs below an expected level.

Under-Emittors of Behavior: those who respond infrequently to conditions within their environments. Characterized as quiet, shy, withdrawn, phobic, and autistic.

Variable-Interval Schedule: pattern of reinforcement in which presentation of reward occurs at random intervals. Contributes to maintenance of learned responses over long time periods.

Variable-Ratio Schedule: pattern of reinforcement in which presentation of reward occurs after differential numbers of correct responses. Contributes to maintenance of learned responses over long time periods.

Visual Learning: discrimination and recall using sight as the sensory mode.

Visual Stimuli: stimuli received through vision.

References

Bandura, Albert, "Social Learning Through Imitation," in *Nebraska Symposium on Motivation,* ed. Marshall R. Jones. Lincoln: University of Nebraska Press, 1962.

Becker, W. C., C. H. Madsen, Jr., Carole Arnold, and Don R. Thomas, "The Contingent Use of Teacher Attention and Praise in Reducing Classroom Behavior Problems," *Journal of Special Education,* 1 (1967), pp. 287-307.

Betts, Emmett A., *Foundations of Reading Instruction.* New York: American Book Company, 1957.

Bijou, S. W. and Persis T. Sturges, "Positive Reinforcers for Experimental Studies with Children — Consumables and Manipulatables," *Child Development,* 30 (1959), pp. 151-70.

Birch, Jack W., *Retrieving the Retarded Reader.* Indianapolis: The Bobbs-Merrill Co., Inc., 1955.

Brown, Clarence W. and Edwin E. Ghiselli, *Scientific Method in Psychology.* New York: McGraw-Hill Book Company, 1955.

Brueckner, Leo J., "The Principles of Developmental and Remedial Instruction," in *Educational Diagnosis,* ed. Guy M Whipple, The Thirty-fourth Yearbook of the National Society for the Study of Education. Bloomington, Illinois: Public School Publications, 1935.

Buros, O. K. (ed.), *The Sixth Mental Measurements Yearbook.* Highland Park, N. J.: Gryphon Press, 1965.

Cruickshank, W. M., *et al., A Teaching Method for Brain-Injured and Hyperactive Children.* Syracuse: Syracuse University Press, 1961.

Dolch, E. W., "A Basic Sight Vocabulary," *The Elementary School Journal,* 36 (1936), pp. 456-60.

Dunn, L. M., "An Overview," in *Exceptional Children in the Schools,* ed. L. M. Dunn. New York: Holt, Rinehart and Winston, Inc., 1963.

Ellis, D. B. and L. W. Miller, "A Study of the Attitudes of Teachers Toward Behavior Problems," *Journal of Educational Psychology,* 27 (1963), pp. 501-11.

English, Horace B. and Ava C. English, *A Comprehensive Dictionary of Psychological and Psychoanalytical Terms.* New York: Longmans, Green and Co., 1958.

Eysenck, H. J., "Classification and the Problems of Diagnosis," in *Handbook of Abnormal Psychology,* ed. H. J. Eysenck. New York: Basic Books, Inc., Publishers, 1961.

Fenichel, Otto, *The Psychoanalytic Theory of Neurosis.* New York: W. W. Norton & Company, Inc., 1945.

Ferguson, Donald G., *Pupil Personnel Services.* Washington: Center for Applied Research in Education, Inc., 1963.

Fernald, Grace, *Remedial Techniques in Basic School Subjects.* New York: McGraw-Hill Book Company, 1943.

Ferster, C. B. and B. F. Skinner, *Schedules of Reinforcement.* New York: Appleton-Century-Crofts, 1957.

Fleishman, E. A. and W. E. Hempel, "Factorial Analysis of Complex Psychomotor Performance and Related Skills," *Journal of Applied Psychology,* 40 (1956), pp. 96-104.

Fries, Charles C., Rosemary G. Wilson, and Mildred K. Rudolph, *Merrill Linguistic Readers.* Columbus, Ohio: Charles E. Merrill Publishing Co., 1966.

Gagne, Robert M. and Noel E. Paradise, "Abilities and Learning Sets in Knowledge Acquisition," *Psychological Monographs: General and Applied,* 75 (1961), pp. 1-23.

Glaser, Robert, "Psychological Bases for Instructional Design," *AV Communication Review,* 14 (1966), pp. 433-49.

Good, Carter, ed., *Dictionary of Education.* New York: McGraw-Hill Book Company, 1959.

Hewett, Frank M., *The Emotionally Disturbed Child in the Classroom.* Boston: Allyn & Bacon, Inc., 1968.

Hilgard, E. R. and D. G. Marquis, *Conditioning and Learning.* New York: Appleton-Century-Crofts, 1940.

Hilgard, E. R. and Gordon H. Bower, *Theories of Learning* (3d ed.) New York: Appleton-Century-Crofts, 1966.

Hill, Winfred F., *Learning: A Survey of Psychological Interpretations*. San Francisco: Chandler Publishing Co., 1963.

Holmes, D. and Lois F. Harvey, "An Evaluation of Two Methods of Grouping," *Educational Research Bulletin,* 41 (1956), pp. 213-22.

Hunter, E. C. "Changes in Teachers' Attitudes Toward Children's Behavior Over the Last Thirty Years," *Mental Hygiene,* 41 (1957), pp. 3-10.

Jastak, J. F., S. W. Bijou, and S. R. Jastak, *The Wide Range Achievement Test: Manual of Instruction*. Wilmington, Delaware: Guidance Associates, 1965.

Jones, Daisy M., "Experiment in Adaption to Individual Differences," *Journal of Educational Psychology,* 39 (1948), pp. 257-72.

Kerlinger, Fred N., *Foundations of Behavioral Research*. New York: Holt, Rinehart and Winston, Inc., 1964.

Kline, Morris, "Intellectuals and the Schools: A Case History," *Harvard Educational Review,* 36 (1966), pp. 505-11.

Kubie, L. S., *Neurotic Distortion of the Creative Process*. Lawrence, Kansas: University of Kansas Press, 1958.

Kuypers, D. S., W. C. Becker, and K. D. O'Leary, "How to Make a Token System Fail," *Exceptional Children,* 35 (1968), pp. 101-10.

Laidlaw, William J., "Teacher-Made Tests: Models to Serve Specific Needs," in *Assessing Behavior: Readings in Educational and Psychological Measurement,* eds. John T. Flynn and Herbert Garber. Palo Alto: Addison-Wesley Publishing Co., Inc., 1967.

Mager, Robert F., *Preparing Objectives for Programmed Instruction*. San Francisco: Fearon Publishers, Inc., 1962.

McCarthy, James J., "An Overview of the I. M. C. Network," *Exceptional Children,* 35 (1968), pp. 263-66.

McKee, Paul G., *The McKee Inventory of Phonetic Skill*. Boston: Houghton Mifflin Company, n. d.

Miller, Neal E. and John Dollard, *Social Learning and Imitation*. New Haven: Yale University Press, 1941.

Osgood, Charles E., "A Behavioristic Analysis," in *Contemporary Approaches to Cognition*, eds. Jerome S. Bruner *et al.* Cambridge: Harvard University Press, 1957.

Otto, Wayne and Richard A. McMenemy, *Corrective and Remedial Teaching, Principles and Practices*. Boston: Houghton Mifflin Company, 1966.

Quay, H. C., "Dimensions of Problem Behavior and Educational Programming," in *Education of the Disturbed and Delinquent Child*, ed. P. S. Graubard. New York: Follet Publishing Company, 1968.

Rachman, S., *Phobias: Their Nature and Control*. Springfield, Illinois: Charles C. Thomas, Publisher, 1968.

Reynolds, G. S., *A Primer of Operant Conditioning*. Glenview, Illinois: Scott, Foresman and Company, 1968.

Saettler, Paul, "Design and Selection Factors," *Review of Educational Research*, 37 (1968), pp. 115-28.

Schachtel, Ernest G., *Metamorphosis*. New York: Basic Books, Inc., Publishers, 1959.

Skinner, B. F., *The Behavior of Organisms*. New York: Appleton-Century-Crofts, 1938.

Skinner, B. F., *Sciece and Human Behavior*. New York: The Macmillan Company, 1953.

Skinner, B. F., *The Technology of Teaching*. New York: Appleton-Century-Crofts, 1968.

Sluckin, W. and E. A. Salzen, "Imprinting and Perceptual Learning," *Journal Experimental Psychology*, 13 (1961), pp. 35-77.

Smith, Karl and Margaret F. Smith, *Cybernetic Principles of Learning and Educational Design*. New York: Holt, Rinehart and Winston, Inc., 1966.

Smith, Robert M. ed., *Teacher Diagnosis of Educational Difficulties*. Columbus, Ohio: Charles E. Merrill Publishing Co., 1968.

Solley, Charles M. and Gardner Murphy, *Development of the Perceptual World*. New York: Basic Books, Inc., 1960.

Staats, Arthur W., *Human Learning*. New York: Holt, Rinehart and Winston, Inc., 1964.

Stephens, T. M., "Organizational Plans for Partially Seeing Children in Grades Five and Six Relative to Language Achievement and

Individual Differences." Unpublished Ph. D. dissertation, University of Pittsburgh, 1966.

Stevens, G. D. and J. W. Birch, "A Proposal for Clarification of Terminology Used to Describe Brain-Injured Children," *Exceptional Children*, 23 (1957), pp. 346-49.

Stevens, G. D., *Taxonomy in Special Education for Children with Body Disorders*. Pittsburgh: University of Pittsburgh Press, 1962.

Stott, D. H. and Emily G. Sykes, *The Child in School (Bristol Social Adjustment Guides)*. San Diego: Educational and Industrial Testing Service, 1967.

Strauss, A. A. and N. C. Kephart, *Progress in Theory and Clinic (Psychopathology and Education of the Brain-Injured Child Vol. II)*. New York: Grune & Stratton, Inc., 1955.

Sutherland, Ivan E., "Computer Inputs and Outputs," in *Information*. San Francisco: W. H. Freeman and Co. Publishers, 1966.

Terman, Lewis M., "Foreword," in *Remedial Techniques in Basic School Subjects*, by Grace Fernald. New York: McGraw-Hill Book Company, 1943.

Thorndike, E. L., "Mental Discipline in High School Studies," *Journal of Educational Psychology*, 15 (1924), pp. 1-22.

Thorndike, E. L., *Selected Writings from a Connectionists Psychology*. New York: Appleton-Century-Crofts, 1949.

Thorndike, E. L. *The Fundamentals of Learning*. New York: Bureau of Publications, Teachers College Press, Columbia University, 1932.

Thorndike, E. L., "The Law of Effect," *American Journal of Psychology*, 39 (1927), pp. 212-22.

Thorndike, R. L., *The Concepts of Over- and Under-Achievement*. New York: Bureau of Publications, Teachers College Press, Columbia University, 1963.

Tiegs, E. W. and Willis W. Clark, *California Achievement Tests*. Monterey, California: California Test Bureau, 1957.

Valentine, C. W., *The Difficult Child and the Problem of Discipline*. London: Methuen Publications, 1965.

Verville, Elinor, *Behavior Problems of Children*. Philadelphia: W. B. Saunders Company, 1967.

Walker, Edward L., *Conditioning and Instrumental Learning*. Belmont, California: Brooks/Cole Publishing Co., 1967.

Washburne, C. W. and L. E. Raths, "The High School Achievement of Children Trained Under the Individual Technique," *Elementary School Journal*, 28 (1927), pp. 214-24.

Wickman, E. K., *Children's Behavior and Teachers Attitudes*. New York: Commonwealth Fund, 1928.

Wilson, John A. and Mildred C. Robeck, *Kindergarten Evaluation of Learning Potential*. New York: Webster Division, McGraw-Hill Book Company, 1965.

Yourman, J., "Children Identified by Their Teachers as Problems," *Journal of Educational Sociology*, 5 (1932), pp. 334-43.

Index